DISCONTINUED

DISCONTINUED

What I Lost and Found
During the Recession

MIRIAM EATCHEL

Full Court Press
Englewood Cliffs, New Jersey

Published in the United States of America
by Full Court Press, 601 Palisade Avenue
Englewood Cliffs, NJ 07632
fullcourtpressnj.com

Visit us at miriameatchel.com

ISBN 978-1-938812-04-0
Library of Congress Control No. 2012956278

*Editing and book design by Barry Sheinkopf
for Bookshapers (www.bookshapers.com)*

Cover photo by Julie Shipman

Cover design by Jamie C. Winters

Colophon by Liz Sedlack

TO MY HUSBAND BRUCE

You deserve me

Acknowledgments

I'd like to thank my drinking buddy, Ken Hyde, and our enabler Gary Hollingsworth. Don Browne and Chelby King have been terrific. I am so grateful to Bob Page and Randy Foster for too many things to list here. Kerry Kadell and the other kind souls who for better or worse encouraged me through this; Marcie Pugh, Kathi Bond, Staci Arnone, Susan Arsht, Alix Railton, Bari Nan Cohen Rothchild, Clare Gilmore, Kelsey Osgood, Jonah Katz, Dedee Caplin, Amanda Boyaki, Mathilde Hoefer, John Niss, and the brutally honest (that is a good thing) Lynne and Eric Slud. The Edish elves were and are amazing, especially Francoise Cooper, Craig Brimmer, Sarah Wigton, Rebecca Ellen, Aaron Danger Sainz, Jamario Head, Lindsey Barnett, Rose Oshman Johnston, Sally Bennett, and Cameron and Kendall Card. Special thanks to my only classy friends, Bob and Tonia Clark. I am also grateful to Leonard McDonald, David Walling, Cathy Kay, Jon Scartlet, Barry Sheinkopf, Julie Shipman, Fred and Josie Nevill, Jamie Winters, and of course, Wynonne Hart. To Tony Arnone: thanks for all the extra pounds. Despite what she thinks, I am very appreciative of my mother, Pat Hutchins. Max and Madeleine Eatchel are the reasons I roll out of bed some days. I am also indebted to The Ted and Carol Levy Fund For Levy Children Who Are Living Up To Their Potential. Believe it or not, I'd also like to thank David Lackey.

Chapter One

"This is no year to gamble!"

December 31, 2008

It has always been my contention that the theory of evolution would not exist if it hadn't been for Wedgwood china. If Charles Darwin's grandfather, Josiah Wedgwood, had not made his fortune in the china business, would Charles have had time to think about natural selection? Would he have had the money to spend five years sailing through South America on the Beagle? Try not to think about the fact that he went on to marry his cousin, Josiah Wedgwood II's daughter Emma. Of course, this helped finance the study of his crazy ideas.

The sordid Darwin/Wedgwood family tree is

floating through my mind as I snowshoe this New Year's Eve, because it beats thinking about my problems. It is a gorgeous Park City, Utah, day. Sunny and crisp. I am alone by virtue of the fact that my six-year-old twins are now too cool to engage in such activities.

Back when they were un-cool, like me, they would say that the sun glistening on the snow looked like diamonds. They were right. On this trail, alone, I have incredible views of mountains on three sides. I could do this every day, and it costs nothing. Being here reminds me of why it is great to be alive—which has not been my fallback feeling of late. The discontinued china business I have worked so hard to make successful for twenty years is on the brink of failure. Meaning, among other things, that the fifteen people who work for me (many of whom have been doing so for much of the last twenty years) may soon be jobless and without health insurance through no fault of their own.

Hearing the snow crunch beneath my feet, I breathe in mountain air and tell myself that I can handle whatever comes next, and so can everyone else.

January 1, 2009

I log onto my computer. New Year's Day is one of the five days a year on which we close.

Nonetheless, I can see that Francoise is working from home. As always, she is doing everything she can to save the business. It seems as if it was yesterday that her seventeen-year-old daughter was born. That day, her husband stole the little bit of money she had hidden under her mattress and used it to buy drugs. I'm sure my memory is somewhat faulty, but I know she had a C-section, and I remember her being gone from work for a few days. But the way I remember it, she came back to work right away, scrubbing dishes and working like a Whirling Dervish.

How she managed to raise her daughter, with no help from the father and without ever complaining, is beyond me. Yaz is brilliant, bilingual, and charming.

Francoise is the hardest worker I have ever met. When she started, the company was called David Lackey Antiques and was owned by—you guessed it, David Lackey. We were small; we sold antiques because they were David's passion, and used china, crystal, and silver because it paid the bills. We hired Francoise to scrub and price the china. It is a labor-intensive business. Each piece has to be checked carefully by a buyer and then washed, dried, and—back then—priced with a hand-written tag. The company was incredibly lean (at the time, so were most of us). We all brought in our old newspapers to wrap customer purchases and our used grocery bags to put them in. We were in the back of a seedy antique mall in Houston, Texas.

David was the kind of boss who would monitor the size of the piece of scotch tape each employee used. I am not exaggerating. On a regular basis, he would explain how much money we could save if each of us could just use a slightly smaller piece of tape. Since the bathroom was some distance away, he'd squirt Windex on his hands instead of walking back to the sink to wash them. His was always the fastest, most logical and efficient, way to drive anywhere, and he never hesitated to tell us so. He was also able to spot the perfect weird antique he knew you would love and save it to give to you for Christmas —and he was invariably right. Maybe that should have been my first clue. It was my first encounter with someone who had an easier time dealing with objects than with people.

January 2, 2009

My father's birthday: For the last several years I have skied with my father on his birthday and he with me on mine. I'll probably be too old to do this before he is. He skis like a teenage boy.

Before we go, I call Don to check in. He runs

the Houston store—does the payroll, advertising, hiring, customer service, pretty much everything. He has been selling china, first with David and then with Edish, for even longer than I have. He wrote lots of the articles on our website, including a passionate discourse entitled *The Cocktail Hour, One Man's Strong and Unyielding Opinions.*[2] And they are. Although he was in his mid-thirties when he wrote the piece, he sounds like he is in his eighties. His great passions in life are mid-century modern design, drinking, and his lovely wife Chelby, I'm not really sure in what order.

To further complicate matters, *I* used to be one of his passions. It was clear to me where I fit in. Once I had to ride in the back seat of my Nissan Sentra with no air conditioning on a trip home from Dallas because a Stickley chair he'd bought that weekend could only fit in the front seat. It was a five-hour drive, and it was my birthday weekend.

The fact that we remained romantically linked for several years after this tells you everything you need to know about my intelligence. Worse than that, we bought a duplex together. After we broke up, we lived next to each other for quite some time, drove to the shop together, spent the day at work with each other, and got to see every person the other dated coming up the walkway. We joked about writing a sitcom about our life called *Side by Side*.

Don annoys many of the people who work with him because he is so consumed by the aforementioned true loves that he often saunters into work quite late. He is also the one who will stay as long as necessary and come in on his days off when the chips are down. He stopped at the shop on his way to his father's funeral to call in payroll. He is smart and hard-working and lazy all at the same time— and never afraid to tell me when I am wrong.

Because he is smart, he has inklings that we may not make it. This has been his livelihood for well over twenty years. Our talk on the phone is pretty much the same as usual: how to increase sales quickly. We have been putting lots of china and crystal on sale by manufacturer, all Wedgwood is 20% off for the next two weeks, that kind of thing. We agree to put Lenox at 30% off to see if it will help. We are desperate for sales.

I ski with my father and try not to think about work. Obviously I fail; my dad takes time from his birthday celebration to tell me that he thinks that it is time to throw in the towel. He points out that I have put a lot of time and money into this venture with nothing to show for it.

Our great relationship is largely based on the fact that we rarely give each other unsolicited advice. I challenge him to a race to lunch, to change the subject and because we both know he can win.

At some point he will become elderly and I will be able to beat him. My life is now reduced to looking forward to my father's aging so that I can gain a sense of accomplishment.

At the end of the day, I talk to my other business partner, Ken. We have been partners since 1999. With the exception of my husband, he is my best friend. This is constantly on my mind, because talking someone into investing a ton of money and a bunch of time in a business that fails is not a particularly smart way to maintain a friendship.

Ken is an eye surgeon who created our entire website, inventory, and point-of-sale system by himself after reading a couple of books on the subject. Seriously. I have to read a couple of books just to bake a cake. And it still falls in the middle.

January 5, 2009

Back at work in the shop in Salt Lake City. Three people work here besides me—Craig, Lindsey, and Jeremy. Craig was not my first employee, but he started a few months after we opened. When he began his Edish career, in 1998, he was on his way to a degree in German at the University of Utah. Smart and hard-working as he was, he never finished the last three classes he needed to graduate. He decided to go back last year and is now in his final semester as a Gender Studies major. Although I don't actually know what that means, he seems enthusiastic about it.

Craig loves china. And order. People, not so much. He is charming when he wants to be, however, so his interactions with customers usually (but not always) go well. His command of obscure facts about various dinnerware patterns is stunning. That, combined with his fastidiousness, makes him a great dish buyer. Used china has to be in perfect condition for a customer to want to purchase it, so the buyers for Edish, who are usually buying from individuals getting rid of their china, need to be the kind of people who can take their time to look over each piece of a huge set with eagle eyes, to make sure there are no chips, nicks, scratches, wear to the gold or silver, or anything else that might make it less than perfect. And they need to verify that the pattern is the exact one. Some crystal patterns have eight or more slight variations—a moss rose, say, instead of a regular rose (the only way I can remember the difference is that a moss rose looks slightly hairy), so the buyers need to be able to look at things very closely. Perfect strangers have stopped me on the street, by comparison, to let me know that my shirt tag is hanging out; I am not a prime candidate for the position of china buyer. I have been very lucky to have had Craig for all of these years.

Love found Craig about a year ago in the form of Ian, an attorney who lives in London. They met online and corresponded for a few months before they decided to trade virtual love for the gamble of actually meeting each other. They both flew to New York. After I insisted, Craig left me all his hotel information and promised to call once he met Ian, to let me know that the man was not a serial killer. Even that phone call was gooey.

Of course it reminded me of when I fell in love with my husband, Bruce. It was disgusting to be around me; all I ever did was talk about him. At the time, Francoise told me it would be nice to hear me answer just one question in a manner that didn't involve Bruce's opinions.

Karmic payback is on my mind as Craig and Ian's romance progresses.

Because of the time difference between London and Salt Lake City, their daily phone call takes place while Craig is still at work. Our shop in Salt Lake City is about 1,500 square feet upstairs, which is where we all work together, with no privacy. This was fine for years, until we had to listen to Craig's side of the conversation. As everyone else in the room can attest (and probably anyone who has ever been around someone newly in love), *Ewwwww.* Once Craig is finally off the phone, we are treated to stories showcasing Ian's brilliance in all matters. Ian and Craig see each other infrequently, in London and Salt Lake City, so it is easy for them to preserve the romantic qualities of their relationship. They never have to fight about whose turn it is to do the laundry.

Not that Bruce and I would ever argue about anything so prosaic. Lindsey, Jeremy, and I, romantics at heart, have bets on how long the relationship will last once Craig and Ian spend more time together.

Lindsey has been working for me for about a year. Also a great buyer, he caught on right away. His last job was as a forensic photographer. Attention to detail is part of who he is.

Jeremy is the shipper. He has only been working with us for a few months. A big bear of a guy with tattoos, a long red beard, two small children, and three teenage step-kids, he has a lot of balls in the air, and yet, any time I ask him how he is, he smiles and says, "Amazing." One of his previous jobs was crime-scene cleanup. Imagine the conversations between a former forensic photographer and a former blood-and-spatter cleanup guy. Our daily chats are quite uplifting.

As our business has deteriorated over the last several months, Jeremy, who needs the money the most, I assume, was one of the first to offer to cut back his hours. Lindsey, Craig, and many people in Houston did the same. They were incredibly flexible; they would leave early if we weren't busy and seemed always to be looking out for each other and the business. When one of them knew another was in a financial bind, they would give that person their hours. It was an awesome thing to watch.

Bob in Houston even offered to work for free. He and his wife Tonia are old friends of mine. He is a retired Shell Oil executive. In 1999, when Ken and I bought into David's business, combining David Lackey Antiques and what was then Chinatown to create Edish, Bob and his wife offered to help with the massive job of inventorying the hundreds of thousands of pieces of china in Houston. She had enough sense not to fall in love with the china business. Bob, on the other hand, did not. He works part time, three days a week. His friends assume that he has fallen on hard times. Watching their faces when they come in to shop is amusing. But Bob just can't seem to help himself. He does it because he loves the products we sell, and the customers, and the people he works with. As is obvious, based on his offer to work for free, he sure isn't doing it for the money. If we were the kind of company that kept statistics, we probably wouldn't be talking about going out of business, and he would be our top salesperson per hour worked. Little old ladies love him, as do all who work with him. He frets over the other employees, does many of their tax returns for free, and once asked me how I had managed to keep so many well-educated, smart people working for me at such low wages for so long. Although he did not coin the phrase, he did not disagree when I told him that some people refer to Edish as the Land of Wasted Potential.

Craig goes out to get lunch, and Jeremy and Lindsey (who have become fast friends) say to each other, "Should we ask her?"

"What?" I say, dreading whatever is coming next.

They ask if I am going to close the Salt Lake store. It is a smart question because, though the rent in Houston is much higher, it would have been best to close the Salt Lake store a long time ago. People in Houston are Southern, and they have oil money; they entertain and can afford to. Ten percent of Utah's population is under five years old. Not big china buyers. Neither are their parents, who often have ten or twelve kids. On the one hand, there are lots of weddings; on the other, china does not seem to be the gift of choice. At least not our kind of china. Weekly, a customer in Utah will ask, "Does this price tag mean $20.00 for *one plate?*"

There were lots of reasons to keep the Salt Lake City store open, but, in hindsight, the overall business would have had a better chance if we hadn't.

We did lots of Internet business, which was easy for me to manage through the store, and we did some local business as well, but the fact that I live in Utah had more to do with keeping it open than anything else.

I expect Jeremy and Lindsey to be angry when they ask whether we will close, since, obviously, it would mean the end of their jobs. They are not. They want me to know that, if that is the plan, they would be happy to pack up our merchandise and drive it to Houston. Although it would be insuring the demise of their own jobs, they offer to do something they know would be incredibly hard.

Eleven years ago Bruce flew to Houston to help me pack up my furniture and a bunch of china I was buying from David to start the business in Salt Lake City. We rented a U-Haul and pulled my Miata behind it. My then-young stepson, Hayden, wrote about this adventure when his teacher asked the students to describe a Utah pioneer in their family. Although she gave him an "A", she made it clear that I was not the kind of pioneer she'd had in mind. Nonetheless, no one knew better than I how hard a trip back to Houston with a bunch of china would be.

I tell them that I am thinking about it, and that I really appreciate them offering. Saying that I don't know what is going to happen next, I promise to keep them posted—and that nothing will happen too fast.

Although I have not been talking to anyone except Ken, David, and Don about doing anything drastic, it is obvious to many of the employees that things are not going swimmingly. The last quarter of the year is usually when we do about half of our business. People are buying to fill out their china to use for Thanksgiving, Christmas, and Chanukah, and they are buying gifts. We sell lots of pretty little figurines and ornaments and other objects that folks collect. Everything is used but in great condition—not just because our buyers inspect it, but because, typically, people take care of expensive things. They only use their china once or twice a year and never let their clumsy brother-in-law help with the dishes. They put their Royal Doulton figurine on the shelf and don't let the maid or their teenager dust it.

The last quarter of 2008 was Recession Central. We had been through lots of recessions before—local ones in Houston when the price of oil was down, national ones; they can be terrific for the china or antiques business. When the economy is bad, people sell beloved china that they never use. And since what we sell is hard to come by, there is always someone who has to have that Lenox Kingsley gravy boat.

This time was different. Scary. Everyone wanted to sell, and no one wanted to buy. We usually put Lenox or Wedgwood or some other good brand on sale in July. No one is thinking about serving their Fourth of July barbecued chicken and potato salad on their fine china. But in the old days, say 2007, if we sent out an email saying that all Lenox was 20% off for two weeks in July, people would scoop up fantastic deals that they knew they would never see when they really needed their china in December. That, and a huge loan from Gary, Ken's significant other and a very close friend of mine, is how we would make it through the summer.

But suddenly, there we were in the fall of 2008 unable to sell anything, even at 30% off. A seven-hundred-point drop in the Dow, and constant panic in the media, had not exactly been inspirational.

We went into 2009 having paid off very little of our debt and having had to discount heavily just to keep our heads above water. It was not a surprise that Edish employees were worried.

January 6, 2009

I am going to Houston next week, so I am doing everything I can to get prepared for meeting with Ken and David to talk about the future of our business. I am also preparing to meet with the staff and my landlady there. The store is much bigger than the one in Salt Lake. Besides Don, Bob, and Francoise, Kerry—the most well-read person on the planet—is there. He has a degree in journalism from the University of Texas, and he's very bright and often cranky. He bears a striking resemblance to Humphrey Bogart (in the later years), although his significant other, Jason, looks nothing like Lauren Bacall.

If he knows you and tells you that you will like a book, he is always right. And he will lend you the book. In hardcover. Kerry, who probably makes less money than your grocery checker, only buys hardcover books. He singlehandedly keeps Amazon in business. He has been working for David and me since 1996. He has been a high-end salesperson at Neiman Marcus and a couple of other expensive local stores. One of the reasons he likes us is that we do not work on commission. This is understandable, given that he was let go from Neiman's after having worked there for six years because he did not meet his commission numbers for two quarters in a row.

There is also Kathi, who has worked for us since 1989. Eighteen when she came for her interview, she wore a black leather motorcycle jacket, had a ton of piercings, and brought a friend. Her friend interrupted the interview to ask for a cigarette. We hired her anyway as our shipper. Now she does our computer networking, database management, and customer emails.

Kathi is another person who always makes sure everything is done right. Just don't ever touch her computer: You might have a germ on your hand. She is loyal and hardworking, and only makes it to work on time if there is a national emergency. But when the server has crashed on her day off, I can call and wake her up and she will be at the shop in fifteen minutes. Best not to talk to her then, though. When my baby brother was eight (he is now in law school), he came to Houston from Connecticut to visit me. He loved Kathi. She had long, beautiful hair and a gorgeous smile. When she took him to play pool, some guy sidled up to the table and offered to show them how the game was played. There were bets placed. That was the day my brother Matt learned the term "pool shark." I am always interested in helping young people improve their vocabulary.

Jamario is now our shipper. Young, handsome, always impeccably dressed, he never makes a mistake. He gets fan mail. When was the last time you wrote to a company to express your gratitude for their shipping? At Christmas, his is the most stressful job in the company. There is no room for error, and customers and our salespeople are hysterical. When I check on him to ask how he is holding up, he always says, "Fine." His last job was in a pawn shop; apparently it was quite intense. And he was shot on a Super Bowl Sunday because he told someone that he did not want to buy drugs from them. Shipping china, and putting up with us, have been a piece of cake for him.

Aaron also works in the back room helping Francoise and Jamario. He just turned twenty. His passion is music, specifically records. Remember those? And playing pranks on Kerry—which I just love. Kerry does not feel the same way. Aaron and Jamario are often looking for ways to torture Kerry, who is not an old man but older than they are by twenty-five years or so. He complains when he can't find something, like the stapler. So when he leaves his desk, they put every stapler they can find on it. They put his favorite coffee cup in a Jell-O mold in the fridge. They change his screen saver from Boy George (don't ask) to Don Rickles when he goes to lunch. There is no good reason why I should find such juvenile stuff so funny, but I do. Having someone around who is young, energetic, and funny lightens the mood and is good for all of us.

Last summer, when I brought my then five-year-olds to Houston, they loved Aaron. He drew them a picture on the day we were leaving and told them not to show it to me. It was of a pet moose he said he would send them. They showed it to every flight attendant, car rental employee, and security person at the airport, telling each of them not to tell me what was in the picture. They cried in the car on the way home and asked, "What do we do when we miss Aaron?" Aaron looks and acts like a big little boy, with a mop of black hair and a near-endless smile.

Rose does displays for us. She can take spit and chewing gum and make them look fantastic. She has a budget of about a hundred bucks a year and manages to come up with all kinds of thrilling displays. She used to do display at the 750-square-foot Ralph Lauren store in Houston, so she says our stuff is easy. I suspect she had a bigger budget at Lauren. Before that she was a substitute teacher. She prefers this job. And she says the pay is about the same, which should tell you everything you need to know about Texas public education. Rose dresses almost exclusively in Ralph Lauren and never has a hair out of place. She is the sort of woman who can wear an antique brooch like it was made for her. I possess no such skill.

Sarah runs the sales floor; she's is a newcomer with about four years in. She comes early, leaves late, is invariably one step ahead of me, and has worked for several other small businesses that have not made it, including a Houston institution called

Don's Records. Maybe china and records are in the same league. Or maybe, as I love to tell her, this is all her fault. Sarah will also not be wearing antique brooches any time soon; her style runs more to t-shirts and shorts than designer outfits.

Rebecca works on the sales floor. She has had several retail jobs over the years selling new china. She and Bob are two of the three people in the Houston store who really love china. If you ask her about a Lenox pattern, she will say, "Oh yeah, that was top seller in 1989 and 1990," or, "That was Tricia Nixon's wedding pattern." Being single and self-supporting, she has been the one most worried about the state of our business. Since she knows that sales are down, she has been asking Sarah daily if she should be looking for a job.

Dale helps on the sales floor during the weekends; his real job is doing display for Dillards. He works at Edish on his days off, is cheerful, and could sell ice to Eskimos. Unfortunately for him, he also loves the products we sell. Practically an indentured servant, he invariably has several layaways that total more than he makes working for us. He creates his own positive cash flow.

The common denominator among the people that I have hired over the years is not a love of china. It is not even retail experience; it is that they care about doing a great job. Figuring out, during the interview process, if they possess this trait is nearly impossible. We have gone through lots of people over the years. Jamario (the Houston shipper) and Jeremy (the Salt Lake shipper) had never shipped china before and didn't care much about dishes. But they get fan mail because they care about doing a great job and making sure it gets done right. Sarah has sold records and rubber stamps. She is great because she understands how to make sure the customer has a wonderful experience.

Early on in Salt Lake City I hired someone with a masters degree who drove a Mercedes. After leaving work at 7:30 p.m. one night because I had to stay late to correct his mistakes, I stopped at the grocery store. I was exhausted. I asked the butcher if he knew where the mustard was. He said, "Sure, I'll show you." He walked me to the mustard aisle. I told him that he was providing outstanding customer service. He came to work for me three weeks later. His children were young, and he was willing to take a pay cut to get daytime hours. China was a complete mystery to him. That we could teach. It is much harder to teach customer service or how to care about your job. He stayed for several years. There are so many books about how to manage people, but it seems to me that the best thing to do is hire smart, decent ones and then get out of their way.

I spend the next couple of days pulling all of our

financial statements together and talking to our incredible bookkeeper, Sally. Sally has the ability to juggle bills and get them paid just in the nick of time, before they turn off the phones or electricity. For us, this has become critical. I am working hard to put together a proposal to save the business that I can pitch to Ken and David.

I am dreading meeting with them, and I am dreading meeting with everyone who works in Houston. My landlady, Wynonne, is a different story. A couple of months ago I got a knot in my stomach every time I thought about her or her husband. Now, I am looking forward to seeing her.

Chapter Two

"Although by 1930 Lenox had developed a highly influential ivory body dinnerware (ca. 1910), received a White House commission and produced many stylish patterns, the firm struggled to stay open during the Depression. The executives took large pay cuts and the workforce took smaller ones."[3]
                    —Charles Venable

January 12, 2009

I am on a flight to Houston.

I like flying because it is usually quiet and I can think. Since I fly out of Salt Lake City, where the dominant population doesn't do any of the following, I usually carry a book of essays with the rather large title *Drinking, Smoking, Screwing*. It cuts down on conversation.

As I work on my proposal to David and Ken, I keep hearing echoes of my husband and my father saying that I should not try to save the business. We have never made much money; I have worked hard. They both tell me that I have great potential and could be doing something else. Something profitable. I think what I always thought at parent-teacher conferences when I was a kid: What if I am living up to my potential? And mostly, this is a terrible time for everyone to be looking for a job. And that so many of these people have worked really hard for a long time.

One possibility is that we could close the Salt Lake City store and cut the percentage of our employees' health insurance premiums that we pay. We pay three-quarters of it now, and that's a big number. The total premium for each employee is $495.00 a month. And we have a $5,000.00 deductible.

We could probably make it if we didn't offer insurance. Lindsey has told me several times that he would rather have a job with no insurance than no job. He's had some kidney problems and now owes thousands of dollars despite the fact that we have this expensive insurance.

We could have a big sale and pay off our debts to reduce interest expenses; I am planning to make a pitch to my landlady in Houston that she cut our rent substantially. Our shop in Salt Lake City is free-standing (and next to a tattoo shop, a much more profitable business than discontinued china). In Houston, we are in a high-end antique mall. My thinking is that we draw in a huge number of customers, and that my landlady will not want lose us during this recession.

I have no idea whether she will go for this, or whether David and Ken will accept the whole proposal. Although we are in trouble, I have some hope that they will agree this new streamlined business model.

Our biggest debts are to Gary and the people we buy our postage from. We have paid off our other major debt.

Every year we get way behind on our Houston rent and pay it off in the fourth quarter. The Antique Pavilion had at one time been owned by two couples—the Kays, who ran it for seventeen years; and the Harts, Jerry and Wynonne. The Harts were majority but mostly silent partners. They were major local celebrities who owned the most important auction house in Houston. Hart Galleries used to be in the space now occupied by the Antique Pavilion, and the Harts have a long-term lease on that space. The location is one of the best in Houston.

The Harts got every significant auction in town—Gov. John Connally, Gene Tierney, various museums, and virtually every affluent estate. Jerry and Wynonne ran the auction house that Jerry's father had started in 1938. The Pavilion was a sideline for them. It provided a way to make money by holding onto their lease while moving their auction house to a bigger, prettier location.

In 2006 they filed for bankruptcy. By the summer of 2008, they had forced out the Kays and were our sole landlords—and they were furious with me because we were so far behind on our rent. Cathy Kay had always just let me pay the back rent at the end of the year, when we had the money, because she knew that our sales always picked up in the fourth quarter.

When I called Jerry Hart to discuss the rent, I knew he was angry. His secretary answered the phone. (When I got to know her better, Wynonne told me she'd actually been the person I spoke to).

She put him on. He asked me how this could have happened yet again and was not happy when I told him that we didn't have the money. He went on to ask if Cathy Kay had told me the previous year that he had laid down the law, and that we were not allowed to get behind again. When I said that she had, I could tell he was surprised that I did not try to blame her. Then he asked me if Ken,

David, and I would sign personally for the rent. I said we wouldn't.

There was a long pause. . .and this man who had lost so much by being on the hook for his business said, "I guess I understand that."

I promised we would work out a payment plan and assured him we would be up to date by the end of the year.

Quite soon thereafter, Wynonne took over dealing with us, and I don't think I spoke to Jerry again. She is larger than life—big blond Texas hair, bright clothes, smokes like a chimney. I have always heard that, when she met Jerry years before, she had been a flight attendant. But she had acquired her auctioneer's license and more or less ran Hart Galleries. Occasionally she could be seen conducting an auction, wearing a hat with a veil and smoking a cigarette with a cigarette holder stuck through the veil. It is very hard to concentrate on bidding the correct amount when you are wondering when the auctioneer is going to immolate herself.

Their auctions were high theater, and they led a swanky life. The wedding they threw for their daughter would later figure in their sentencing hearing. Needless to say, I was not invited to the wedding. Six hundred of Houston's glitterati at the nicest restaurant in town: It was quite a soirée.

By the time I was dealing face to face with

Wynonne in October 2007, their business had been through bankruptcy, and they had been arrested, had their mug shots in the paper—the whole nine yards. The news reports said that they'd been arrested for not paying consignors for things that sold at auction.

Somehow, she was still intimidating.

Virtually everyone in the building was angry with her for having forced out the Kays. David yelled at her in front of a group of people. Calmly, she told him that if he didn't like it, he could move out, *now*, a very gutsy move in the middle of the nastiest recession most of us have ever lived through. Her message was clear. Of about fifty dealers, one indeed did move out. It was not David. She is tough.

Anyway, I had to go to her and tell her that, although we owed her tens of thousands of dollars, we couldn't yet pay. The economy was scary as hell, and we both knew that, though we had been able to pay up every other year, there was no certainty we'd be able to so this year. Knowing better than anyone what a house of cards we could be building, there was a very real chance that she could kick us out. It would not be easy to move two million dollars' worth of china in the middle of the night.

I very nervously suggested we go have a drink. She readily agreed. We went across the street and ordered Bellinis. Why not? I thought. If I'm going down, it might as well be in style.

I told her quite straightforwardly that we didn't have the money and couldn't borrow it. I said that we would pay her every week until we were caught up, though I had no idea how we were going to manage that. Three Bellinis and a pack of cigarettes later (only she was smoking), she agreed. Throughout the talk, her phone rang every five minutes—one attorney or another wanting to speak to her. She was just hell on wheels, puffing away, yelling at people over that phone.

Afterwards, we kept in touch—the first few times because I had to skip a payment. She was furious. We put all kinds of things on deep discount. Wedgwood went on sale for 30% off, something we had never done before, much less in the fall. Nevertheless, it was just shocking; we could not sell anything. People were terrified to spend money.

By discounting like crazy, though, calling our best customers and selling things cheaper than ever before and doing anything we could think of, we managed to scrape through and get the back rent paid off. With the exception of the few missed payments, I had kept my word.

AFTER THAT MEETING, anytime I was in Houston, I would pop into her office to give her our latest updates and get hers. One time, she told me that she and her husband had decided to plead guilty to one of the counts against them in exchange for getting the others dropped. I was shocked, because she had sworn repeatedly to me that they were not guilty, but I assumed she knew what she was doing. Telling me that a judge would sentence them, and that they had a few months until that happened, she insisted that she didn't expect to go to jail.

All of this is swirling around in my mind now as I weigh the prospect of suggesting a huge rent reduction to her. She may be receptive to it, because she is a smart businessperson and we do bring in a lot of traffic.

I am not even sure I can get *Ken and David* to agree to this new business model, but it is the only way that I can think of to save everyone's jobs. My father and husband are right to say that it may be time for me to throw in the towel; but I don't want to. I think about how hard it will be for everyone to find a job right now.

When I arrive at the shop, the first thing I notice is how great it looks. Rose has done fabulous displays. Many people hug me. I have a meeting with Ken and David that evening and a management meeting with Don, Kerry, Francoise, and Sarah the next day.

When I speak to an employee I know moderately well but not intimately, she asks if she should be looking for a job. I tell her I am honestly not sure.

She tells me that she is so concerned because, at one time, she was homeless, and, though it was only for a brief period, it was the worst and scariest time in her life.

Dumbfounded, I struggled with how to respond. I had no idea. She's a smart, funny, well-educated person. I tell her I will do my best but cannot guarantee that we will stay open, and I suggest that she indeed look for another job.

Suddenly the stakes seem higher than ever.

Worn out but not done for the day, I go to Ken's house to meet with him and David. The last time we all met was in early December. They said then that it was time to think about closing, but that we could table the discussion until we saw what kind of Christmas we'd had.

During that trip, David and I had also met at 59 Diner (a Fifties-style eatery near Highway 59) for breakfast. He told me then that he just thought it was time to move on. He also gave me a coffee-table book entitled *Domestic Art* as a Christmas present. Hot off the presses, it featured lots of fabulously decorated homes in Texas, including his. The photos of his townhouse were terrific, though they didn't do it justice. Referring to his presence on the cult hit *Antiques Roadshow* for the last thirteen years, it also calls him a renowned china authority and madcap. Only a few rooms of his townhouse are featured.

David's entire house brims with fabulous antiques and art, all placed perfectly. Each wall is covered with terrific paintings from virtually every period. One bathroom features small Texas bluebonnet oil paintings. Another room has antique shell dishes from the late 1700s. Upstairs you will find a George Nakashima table once owned by Andy Warhol, a giant ceramic lobster in the bathtub, and the best collection of books about antiques that I have ever seen. If you went to his house for dinner every Sunday for the next year, you would see some fabulous thing you had not noticed before every single time.

David does *stuff* quite well. And he really tries with people. Last summer, he invited my kids over to feed his snapping turtles. They were at once terrified and thrilled. When my husband and I got married, David and Ken waltzed with each other at our wedding; the look on my grandmother's face was priceless. David gave us the very rare ice tongs in our silver pattern. I still use a giant black Italian vase that he brought to a party I threw sixteen years ago, overflowing with gladiolas.

DAVID HAS BEEN an appraiser on *Antiques Roadshow* since its inception. I wrote the initial letter to them (from him) asking that he be considered, after the Harts suggested him. The show was filming in Houston at the time. Watching it become popular, and hearing the salacious antiques and appraiser gossip over the years, has been fun; and the whole thing has been a dream come true for David. In spite of the fact that they have to pay their own way (which has always surprised me), he has been thrilled to be a part of flying around the country and telling people whether their treasures are valuable or not. He even has a few groupies, something he finds amusing.

WE MEET. I propose closing the Salt Lake store (and show how much money that will save), cutting insurance benefits (I am still worried that lots of people will not be able to afford health care anymore, but Lindsey's words about wanting to have a job more than insurance echo in my head), having a big sale to reduce inventory and pay off debt (which will cut interest payments out of our monthly expenses), and cutting anything else I can think of. I say I am going to meet with Wynonne in the morning to see if I can get our rent reduced, which I know is a long shot. David rails on about how stupid and mean Wynonne is.

Ken asks if I have the fire in my belly to do all of this work. Closing the Salt Lake store, moving the inventory to Houston, changing how we do lots of things, all of that will be gut wrenching. I do feel a fire in my belly, but I am pretty sure it is indigestion. David says he does not want to continue in the business but agrees that we can talk again after I speak to Wynonne.

January 13, 2009

Dreading this talk with her, I sit down in her smoky office and shoot the breeze for a few minutes, then say, "We're not going to be able to renew our lease at the end of March. The only way we can stay is if you consider a substantial reduction in rent. We bring a lot of people in the door. We're your biggest tenant, and we have the least desirable space."

I breathe. I wonder if she is going to haul off and slap me.

After yet another big drag on her cigarette, she starts asking me detailed, smart questions about our financials. She goes on to tell me that we shouldn't be in the Pavilion at all, that our business plan doesn't make sense, that we can't afford a high-end retail space, that we should be in a warehouse space, and that she'd better help me find it because I am a terrible negotiator.

Whatever response I expected—yelling or a counter-offer—it was not this, which goes completely against her self-interest. Never one to turn down assistance, I ask if she can help right away. Telling me that, when they had to "downsize," she had looked at every warehouse space in town, she says she knows what is available and what is well priced in good neighborhoods. We talk about how, if we move to a warehouse, we will lose many of our high-end customers, but how some will still shop with us, our mail order business will remain, and we will slash our expenses.

The next thing I know, she is on the phone with someone, saying, "Yes, we want to look at it today. How about half an hour? And give me your best price—don't give me any of this triple-net bullshit." She drops everything, and we go. Taking my rental car, she drives all over town and smokes while doing it. I think about the rules I am breaking while doing this and notice what a prude I am.

While we are driving around, looking at various spaces—several of which make sense for us—she asks more questions about the fundamentals of our business. Then she tells me to be careful, saying that they went bankrupt trying to save their employees' jobs. Although I know the story is more complicated than that, I also know there is some truth to it.

She also pushes me to think about what I want to be doing with my time. Reminding me that my children are young, she says this is a time that I will never get back with them, and that mine is a hard business that is not profitable. Think carefully about how you want to be spending each day, she says, because life is short. This is a woman who has just pled guilty to felony misappropriation of funds, has a business to run, and should be taking care of her legal defense and her business instead of dropping everything to spend the day finding her biggest tenant someplace to move. She makes me swear never to tell Jerry that she is doing this.

Back at the shop, I tell Don what has transpired. Her response shocks him as well. On and off for the past year or so, he and I have been looking at various buildings that Edish might buy. We never really thought much about renting, because the idea of moving hundreds of thousands of pieces of china someplace and then having to move them again in a few years, or ever, seemed so daunting. But we are reconsidering. It beats closing.

Ken wants to meet at his house. I am emotionally exhausted. I must look great slumped over on the couch, because when he comes home, he says, "You look terrible. Is it because you're a big failure?"

In fact that is exactly why. He tells me later that he didn't mean it the way it sounded. I'm sure he meant Big Failure in a *nice* way.

We talk about Wynonne and my day; he is

blown away by how great she was and says he is willing to consider moving to a warehouse. Don and I will go look at some other rental or purchase possibilities tomorrow, and then Ken and I will re-group.

Curling up in bed, I take an Ambien but still can't sleep. To cheer myself up, I pick up a book in Ken and Gary's guest room and read it cover to cover. It is called *The Pilot's Wife* and is about a woman whose husband, an airplane pilot, dies in a crash; it turns out he has had another wife and child for several years.

Just what I need.

January 14, 2009

I pull the covers over my head and wonder what would happen if I stayed in bed all day. I get up and drink tons of coffee—on top of Ambien. Now I really *do* have a fire in my belly.

Don and I have several appointments to look at warehouses. One looks promising, so Ken agrees to meet us there. It is not. After he leaves, Don and I go have lunch at Goode Company BBQ, a uniquely Texan place where businessmen and women sit outside at long picnic tables, elbow deep in ribs covered with sauce, accompanied by jalapeño corn bread. You can order potato salad or beans or dirty rice; just don't try to order a real salad or anything else green. The employees all wear t-shirts that read *You might give some thought to thanking your lucky stars you're in Texas*. Although I can remember lots of times when I thought that sentiment was profound, I am not feeling much like I have any lucky stars at all.

Don knows that it is not looking good for Edish. I tell him everything. If you ever have a secret, don't tell me. Some people still call me "the mouth of the South," and I haven't lived in the south for over ten years. But feel free to tell Don. Except for the thing about not getting to work on time ever, Don would make a great secret agent. He will never share a confidence, and he likes his martinis shaken, not stirred.

I tell him that David seems very gung-ho to close, and that Ken is willing to continue but only if we radically change the business model. He already knows that David, Ken, and I each own a third of the business, but that I also owe David money (part of my share of the purchase price of the china assets from David Lackey Antiques in 1999 was a loan from David, to be paid back out of my share of the profits from the business. Since there have rarely been any profits, I have not paid much back). David is legally entitled to more of my shares of the company instead of payment, but he has never exercised that option. Who wants more shares of an unprofitable company when you are accumulating interest?

Don has been hustling, putting things on sale, trying anything he can to save Edish for so long that it is hard to tell him that it might not work. He is angry. He tells me that this job used to be fun but hasn't been for a long time, which reminds me of something Cathy Kay said to me when our in-store sales in Houston started to crater. She said that, when Don and I were on the sales floor, it had been much more fun to shop at Edish. We were always laughing and joking with each other and with customers. Her remark made me giggle, because I remembered her complaining about how loud we laughed, and how inappropriate it was, back when.

Part of me feels defensive, and part of me truly understands. Don has been doing this for even longer than I have. He has put a lot of himself into this business. It is not the relaxing lunch I am hoping for. We both go back to the shop cranky. A couple of hours later I get this email from him (I know he is contemplating the loss of his job, the only one he has had since he was in his early twenties, so I am taken aback by the tone):

> *This isn't going to make a difference in your decision about things, but I thought I should have made a couple of additional com-*

ments at lunch. (I didn't respond properly or say exactly what I meant.) It was kind of hard to take it all in and know exactly how to respond at the time.

Anyway, regarding what I said about not having fun for awhile. . .just so you know, I need to qualify that. Overall I have had lots of fun. We have had some amazingly varied and interesting people come through our doors and our lives here over the years, customers and co-workers and other dealers many of whom became "family". I appreciate the opportunity I have had to get to know people here the way I have. Learning about others in an intimate way can teach you so much about life and about yourself. I have also been able to learn so many different things about a small business. . .pretty much every aspect. Most of which is not taught in business texts and classes, or at least it used to not be. And mostly I appreciate the flexibility that Edish has extended me, so that I could put in my hours but also pursue my many other interests over the years. Speaking of interests, to be able to learn about and collect vintage china and crystal while I was working here was monumentally important to me. . .no kidding. When I think back about it all, I will always remember the good times, and there were lots of them. So yes, I have had quite a bit of fun *regardless of the pressure and the stress that came with the job.*

> *As for your comment about feeling like a fail-ure: You are anything but a failure, Miriam. I have learned so much from you over the years that I wouldn't know where to begin to thank you. I know you have had a similar impact on lots of the other people who have worked here and who con-tinue to work here. Even if Edish "rarely made a profit," many of us benefited greatly in our per-sonal lives from coming to our jobs here. I think you are smart enough (and your ego is big enough) to know that there are some remarkable things about Edish, regardless of the bottom line. Be proud of the work you have done.*

This wasn't even the first time this week that someone has been worrying about my feelings when they should have been thinking about them-selves—Wynonne, Ken, and now Don.

In spite of the fact that I had a morning meet-ing scheduled with the entire staff, and that I needed to be ready and composed, I went to my friends Leonard's and Dave's that night for mar-tinis, wine, and good cheer. Don and Chelby went, too.

Leonard is an old friend. He used to work for me when I ran David Lackey Antiques and later at

Edish in Houston. After attempting to go out on his own as a mid-century modern dealer and antique mall owner, he is now working part time for David again. As collectors of mid-century modern art, furniture, and decorative objects, he and Dave have a house that is a constantly changing bonanza of super-cool stuff. They probably have thirty paintings hanging on the wall at any given time, and they have moved them and hung new ones every time I visit. They do the same with their furniture. Each time I go to their house, there is something new, and everything is arranged differently. They are wonderful hosts; I always feel relaxed when I am there.

Leonard, Don, another friend, Randall, and I used to spend lots of time together. Getting to hang out with them is like coming home. Now Dave and Chelby are part of that, too. Leonard used to have atrocious taste in men. One day I suggested that gay bars in the wee hours of the morning might not be the best place to search for a life partner. But, though I wish I could take credit for him finding Dave, he did it on his own, at a gay softball league, the same year that Leonard was Mr. November in the league's calendar. Did I mention that Leonard is gorgeous?

This is the kind of friend Leonard is: Last year for Leonard's fiftieth birthday, Dave rented a house on the beach in Galveston in January and had a huge party. There was Veuve Clicquot, homemade gumbo, crab, shrimp, just wonderful Texas Gulf food and drink (okay, only Texans think that Veuve is a *Texas* drink). There were even M&Ms that read *Happy Birthday, Leonard*. Every detail was terrific. I stayed the night, as did about ten other people. The next morning, a group of us took a walk on the beach. I apologized for the way I looked, what with being hung over and not having showered.

Leonard said, "You look like a movie star." And he made me feel that way. Let me assure you that, if I had looked like a movie star, it must have been Shelly Winters. I was thirty-five pounds overweight, unshowered, and green from too much drinking the night before.

Last summer, during the aforementioned trip to Houston with my twins, Leonard, Dave, Don, Chelby, and I took my kids on an all-day fishing and crabbing trip to a place since destroyed by Hurricane Ike. We found a rickety old pier, and Leonard and Dave and Don showed the kids how to catch crabs with raw chicken legs, how to bait a hook, how to catch fish, how to throw said fish back into the water. We all spent the night in Galveston, and Don taught the kids how to make sausage biscuits for breakfast, how to jump waves in the Gulf of Mexico, how to play so hard that you just fall into bed. All four of the adults were so patient and loving, it was the highlight of my kids' year.

SO I RELAXED at Leonard and Dave's house, drank some wine (Dave collects wine, and he has so much that his wine refrigerator is making the back of his house sink), and did not talk about work or my upcoming day one bit.

January 15, 2009

We have a 9 a.m. store meeting. David has agreed that I can try to put something together to save the company. But it is also not his first choice. I don't want to give anyone false hope, and I don't want to scare people into quitting if we can save the company.

I talk about trying some bigger sales and doing what we can to pay back some debt.

During the meeting, Rebecca asks if we are going to make it and whether she should be looking for a job. Saying that I am hoping that we do, and that we are doing everything we can think of, I tell her that I can't promise we can make it work. It is a grim conversation.

Next, I meet with the managers and tell them to keep it quiet but that we are going to look into moving if we can find an appropriate space. Sarah and Francoise proceed for the next month to tell Don and me about every place they drive past that is for rent or sale.

On my way to the airport, Don comes with me as far as the Galleria (one of the biggest and most opulent shopping malls ever—Neiman's, Saks, Macy's, Nordstrom, Mont Blanc, Tiffany, etc.). I am desperate to get a birthday present for my stepmother. We are shell shocked and barely say anything. Virtually everything in every store is on sale, and there are no shoppers. Walking through a huge shrine to capitalism with gleaming purses, shoes, dresses, and shiny objects, with no one buying a thing, is eerie.

That night I get home and pick up my kids from my father and stepmother's house. Bruce is in San Diego for work.

January 16, 2009

After taking my kids to school, I get on another airplane to meet Bruce in San Diego for a party at his boss's house. His boss, Jim, and Jim's wife Elke, graciously asked us to stay with them. This would be a smart time to be a cheerful party spouse, but since I feel like I am wrapped in a depressive shroud, it is not in the cards. The event is casual. I have not lived in California since first grade, so I do not realize what that means and show up in a black-and-red wrap dress, black tights, and heels. I am the only person who is not in jeans. This is the high point of my evening.

January 17, 2009

Over breakfast, Jim, a Harvard MBA with the bouncy energy of a six-year-old boy, talks to me about ways to save my business. He has a bunch of ideas, but it is hard to get around the fact that the business model is old fashioned. These days, Internet businesses make money because they don't invest in inventory. They drop-ship everything. In the discontinued china business, though, you have to have a ton of inventory so you have what someone wants when they want it. And it is labor- intensive inventory. Someone has to work hard to offer a price on it; someone else has to buy it, clean it, shelve it, write to customers that we have it, just to get to the point where we sell it and ship it or carry it out the door to someone's car. Yes, we still do that.

When I tell Jim that a big part of why I believed in this venture was that I watched my biggest competitor (Replacements, Ltd.) grow his store from a hobby into a $70-million-a-year used dish business, he points out there are many companies that size who do not make a profit. This does not cheer me up.

Nor does waving to the beach on the way home. San Diego is gorgeous, and everyone I see looks happy and sun-dappled. I hope we don't have to move here for Bruce's job. I would never fit in.

January 20, 2009

Carol, my stepmother, calls to see if she can come over to watch the inauguration, since she and my father do not have a TV. I tell her that I have to go to work, but that she is welcome to come to my house. She rightly points out that I will never have an opportunity to see this again. Not to mention that I am finding it depressing to be at the shop.

I cannot believe it when I hear our new president talk about self-sacrificing Americans who cut back on their own hours to save their co-workers' jobs. Rebecca, and Kerry and Jeremy, have all done that. Bob offered to work for free. I think of all these bright, hard-working people who have toiled for years at a low-paying job because they like what they are doing and whom they are working with. It used to seem unique, but now I wonder if it is. Most people want to work hard, do a good job, and be treated fairly, I think.

There are so many moving things about the inauguration, but my favorite is Aretha's hat.

January 26, 2009

I stay home from work to call Replacements, Ltd. to ask them what they would pay for our website and mailing list. This needs to be done today, because I told Ken and David that I would, and Ken and Gary are coming to visit tomorrow. My incredible time-management skills are on display yet again.

Replacements, Ltd. practically invented the discontinued china business. Bob Page, the president, was an accountant who turned selling used dishes out of his garage into a huge business.

When we started Edish, Replacements was not selling on the Internet and had no plans to. I thought that, if we could even get a small percentage of their business, we could be happily profitable. Many people said that we were crazy, that discontinued china customers would never buy online. Our typical customer was an older woman, and back in the late 1990s the conventional wisdom was that only young people would spend money on the Internet.

Ken and I worked hard to make our website easy to use. Hundreds of people told us that ours was the first Internet purchase they had ever made. Our prices were great, and for a couple of years we were one of the few china matchers that sold online. Of course, the second Replacements decided to sell from their website, they sold more online in a month than we did in a year.

Last fall I called and talked to Page to see if he would consider buying Edish. First, I did all the laundry and dishes in the house for two days, getting my courage up to make the call. Over the years, we have done lots of business with Replacements, and I have met Page at their warehouse in North Carolina. He also has twins, and we have exchanged little gifts for the kids at Christmastime. But he is still the president of a company that does $70 million in sales yearly, and I am president of a company that never reached $2 million.

When I finally did get to talk to him he was incredibly gracious and charming. We spoke for an hour. If I had been him, I would not have spent an hour talking to me.

A huge part of the discontinued china business has always been the ability to buy the merchandise. If you can buy "good" patterns, you can sell them. "Good" patterns are not necessarily good-*looking*. In fact, some are hideous. But they are desirable. What sells is not just what is fashionable at the moment; it is also about how long ago it was discontinued and how popular it was when it was sold originally, and about factors unknown, like current trends. But buying has always been key.

Houston is a great place to buy china, and I knew that Page was aware of that. He has football field-size warehouses in North Carolina. Over the years we have competed to buy desirable sets of china, and we have been able to win when people were selling things in Houston. My thought was that perhaps he would consider buying Edish as his first satellite location largely because of our buying power.

When I asked if I could fly to North Carolina to discuss this possibility, he said, "Sure."

The next day Randy Foster, one of his VPs, called to say that I was welcome to come, but that it was very unlikely that they would be interested, and they hated to see me waste a trip. The man could not have been nicer. He went on to say that they were experiencing the same issues with the economy that we were; china-buying opportunities were everywhere. When he asked, I told him that I wasn't sure what we would do next. We agreed to keep in touch.

So I call Randy when I want to get an offer on our mailing list, web site, and 800 phone numbers. Again, he is very kind. He asks me what I am going to do personally, and if I intend to stay in the china business. I tell him that I have no idea what I am going to do next, but that, whatever it is, it will be something that has no inventory. He laughs. Sort of. And says that he will get back to me with an offer.

January 27, 2009

Ken and Gary arrive; Ken snowboards, and Gary snowshoes and cross-country skis. Our house is small, with a tiny guest bedroom right across from the kids' room. Not exactly the glamour that Ken and Gary are used to at their fabulous modern house. Nor the quiet. My kids think Gary is their best friend. Being a good sport about this, he lets them "do" his hair, plays endless games with them, cooks with them, laughs at their jokes, and tells them not to call him Uncle Gary. Cousin Gary is fine. Just not "Uncle"—we wouldn't want anyone to think that he is old enough to be their uncle.

After picking them up at the airport, we go straight to the Canyons Ski Resort—Gary to snowshoe, and Ken and I to ski and snowboard. Ken graciously does not bring up the fact that I talked him into starting this business, and that he has now invested a ton of time and money in something that is about to end with nothing to show for it. Must be good breeding. I can think of virtually nothing else. We both manage to avoid the topic for most of this trip.

January 29, 2009

Ken and I are having an epic ski day. Deep powder, sunshine. . .as we come off the lift, he takes a little spill. He says he is okay, but I can tell he's not. We gingerly make our way down the mountain, and that is the end of Ken's snowboarding for the season. He fell on his shoulder and is in immense pain; I suggest he see a doctor. His curt reply: "I *am* a doctor." So is Gary. But neither one of them knows any more about shoulders than I do. He spends the rest of the trip with his head in a book, replying to all questions with one-syllable answers. This does wonders for our relationship.

January 30, 2009

Randy calls back with an offer, but Gary and I are off cross-country skiing in the Uinta Mountains. I asked Randy to call me at home, so that I didn't have to try to discuss the issue at the shop, where I have no privacy. My mother-in-law, who is babysitting, pries to find out who Randy is and what he wants. I think she might have been some kind of interrogator in World War II, because she is very good at it. But Randy doesn't give up any info.

He has left for the day by the time I get back from my adventure with Gary—because neither Gary nor I wanted to be the first to say that it was time to turn around. I have an advantage, because I am used to the altitude, but Gary is more buff than Brad Pitt. I am worn out and have blisters by the end of the day.

February 1, 2009

When I take Ken and Gary to the airport, we do not exactly have a long emotional good-bye because I will be staying with them in Houston in two days, which will kind of be D-Day for Edish. I feel sick thinking about it. Ken lets me know that he does not really see a way to make Edish work. He is willing to look at my proposal, but he wants me to know that he is not hopeful. This does not make me feel any better.

February 2, 2009

Randy calls back and makes a very fair offer for our website and mailing list, although I was hoping for more. He says he would be happy to expedite the process if we need the money right away. Thanking him, I tell him that we are not ready to sell yet, partly because we plan to use the list in the coming months to sell our inventory. Of course, I also know that this will allow me to shop our list around a bit. I assume he knows this as well, which is part of why he would like to get us locked in.

Tomorrow I am off to Houston. As I tuck my kids into bed, my daughter throws her arms around my neck and begs me not to go. I ask her, "Would you like me to figure out a way to stop going to Houston?" Fantastic. Now I am sowing seeds of guilt in my six-year-old daughter, so that someday I can say, "Mommy closed her business because you didn't like her leaving you." Not only am I a spectacular business failure, but now I will have to give back that Mother-of-the-Year award.

Speaking of mother of the year, after the kids are in bed, I drive to the airport to pick up *my* mother, who is coming to help Bruce with the kids while I am away. The first thing she says is, "You haven't called me in six weeks."

I snap that I have a few things on my plate right now. She then goes on to tell me a story that she told me last week over the phone, when I called her.

Chapter Three

*"By the end of this century, six billion
people will be living on this small planet.
Elegance and style, not just superficially
displayed but as a manner of living, are
necessary for harmonious existence in a
crowded world."* [4]

—Emilio Pucci

February 3, 2009

On the plane to Houston, I think about how this
is going to be one of the most important weeks of
my life. All of my ducks need to be in a row if we
are going to save the business. The Edish financials,
and a list of all the things we could cut, are with me.
Frankly, I am guessing about how many sales we
would lose if we close the Salt Lake store and move

to a cheaper location in Houston. I am trying to be conservative but not so conservative that Ken and David won't want to do it.

Unfortunately I am also bringing a *New Yorker* magazine. Clearly it is desperately important for me to read about the Obamas' inauguration parties—especially the one held by Russell Simmons and Magic Johnson. (I believe the Obamas did not attend.) And I must know about Booker T. Washington. And Caroline Kennedy's ill-fated attempt to become a senator from New York. I may not have a talent for running a business, but I am a master at procrastination.

Finally, I get down to work. Although I have a workable proposal, I also meditate upon what to say to customers and employees if we *do* decide to close. My meeting with Ken and David is scheduled for 6 p.m. tonight.

When I get to the shop from the airport, everyone is very subdued. They know something is up, because my visits to Houston never come this close together. No one looks very happy to see me. *I* am not happy to see me.

Walking up and down aisles filled with stacks and stacks of china, I think back to the week that the deal to combine David Lackey Antiques and what was then Chinatown (our store in Salt Lake City) went through ten years ago. I remember being right here then, thinking of all the possibilities. At that time, none of the inventory was computerized. Many of the Edish employees had never even *used* a computer. Picturing Francoise in tears (I've only ever seen that once), saying that she would never be able to use a computer, makes me smile, since she is now a whiz at it. At the time I just knew that we were going to have discontinued china shops all over the country someday. We were all going to make a ton of money. Everyone who worked hard would share in our success. Feeling so far from that hopefulness, it seems as if I am walking through a deep, dark cloud.

When I stop in to Wynonne's office, she gives me a pep talk. Since she has a few other things going on, I find this very sweet.

Ken calls me to say that maybe he and I should talk first before meeting with David, because maybe we can save the business after all. Maybe I misunderstood his pessimism.

I call David and reschedule our meeting.

KEN COMES HOME, looks at my proposal and says, several martinis later, that he thinks it could work. He thinks we would have to eliminate my job, too. It might mean that I am out of a job and we would have to let go more people than I would like, but we could make a go of it. I have no idea what changed his mind, but I am happy to have an opportunity to try to make it work.

February 4, 2009

I get up and call Don first thing to tell him that Ken is more willing than I thought to give it a try. He needs to drop everything and find us a cheap warehouse fast, while I am meeting with Ken and David. We can go look at a few things this afternoon if he can set it up. For the first time in months, I am filled with the sense that my plan might work. It feels great. The deep dark depression I felt yesterday has lifted.

DAVID AND KEN and I meet at Ken's house to go to an early lunch at a dive Mexican restaurant. We drive together. On the way over, Ken (who is never confrontational) says to David that he is very upset about the fact that, if we close the business, it will nullify David's agreement not to buy and sell china on the side. This means that David can go back into the china business and profit from insisting that we close. Ken does not say that he thinks that this is David's motivation for wanting to close Edish, but it is implied.

This, of course, had been on my mind as well, but I had no idea Ken was planning to bring it up. The air suddenly feels thick, and the car seems quite small.

Sitting down at the restaurant, David looks us both square in the eye and says that he has absolutely no intention of going into the china business ever. He goes on to be very specific. He says he doesn't want to be a china matcher. The business is too hard. If he buys the set to get the dinner plates to sell, he then gets stuck with the cups and saucers because no one wants those. He says that he is happy selling antiques, and that is that.

I have known him well for over twenty years and Ken for almost that long. Although I am having lots of feelings about David and Edish at this moment, none of them are about his integrity. I have no reason to doubt him.

He goes on to say that he is totally unwilling to stay in the china business. Saying that he cares about me deeply, he says that I might be able to do something to salvage my life if we get out now. He acts like he is doing me a favor.

Ken suggests to him that maybe Ken and I can buy David out, or that David can take his third of the merchandise and we can take our two-thirds and part ways. David says that he doesn't want to do that but agrees that we can think about it and try to pull something together in the next day or two.

Because I am curious, and because there seems to be nothing left to say, I ask about the status of his case against X, his former employee. In 1999, when we combined the two businesses, there were several employees I wanted David to keep for his antiques business because I did not want them working for me. One was X. David was very happy to do that, because he was crazy about X and wanted him to do all of his eBay business.

I couldn't put my finger on what bothered me about him, but it didn't matter because David wanted him. A few months later, X was hauled out of David's shop in handcuffs. He told David that it was all a big mistake, that someone else had stolen electronic equipment from his former employer and blamed him. While he was incarcerated for several months, David held his job for him because David believed in him.

X came back to work, set up and ran David's eBay business, and made David a bunch of money, or so we heard. He was always arrogant about his eBay abilities and most everything else. I did not have much contact with him after that. He married a lovely woman, worked for David, and made films starring David's boyfriend, and Leonard, and various other people I was friends with. Last year, David and his boyfriend, and Leonard and Dave, went with X and his wife, and another couple, on a vacation to Napa. Obviously, they were close. It always struck me as a little odd that X drove a car nicer than David's, but I figured either that his wife did well or that David was compensating him well for doing such a good job.

DAVID COULD BE rude and curt with his employees, but I had always heard that he was great to X. Over the years, several of David's other employees mused to me that X was always treated like the golden child; resentment abounded.

A couple of months ago, David called me to ask if he could hire our eBay person to help him with a problem. This was big news, since X had always been held up as the ultimate eBay expert. David went on to say that X was no longer working for him, and that he was not allowed in the building. He told me that he was not supposed to discuss it.

Then he did. It appeared that X had been funneling money from David's eBay sales into his own PayPal account, perhaps for years, perhaps into the six figures.

I was utterly shocked—not that X could have *done* such a thing, although I never would have guessed it, but that it could have happened to *David*. When I worked for him years ago, Don and I balanced his checkbook every night, whenever he went out of town. It had to be perfect. He was the kind of person who always knew every penny that was coming in and going out. He was, after all, the

Scotch tape monitor.

So, at lunch, I ask how the case was proceeding. He tells us that, although he has turned everything over to the DA, he has also hired an attorney to expedite the process. He says it is just a matter of time before X is arrested. They have subpoenaed X's PayPal records, and they are sure that all of the evidence will be right there. Lunch ends on that happy note.

Ken and I have a conversation about the possibility of having a sale big enough to buy out David, since he seems so intractable about not wanting to be in the business.

Don has found a warehouse for us to look at, so Ken, Don, and I go look at it. It is in a great location, but it has too many problems. Ken goes to work, and Don and I go look at another warehouse we can afford. We stand outside and count three Harris County prison buses driving by in ten minutes. There are also lots of people who appear to be homeless hanging around. He loves the building because you can see downtown from it. Sadly, I tell him that I can't picture our customers driving their Cadillacs into this neighborhood.

IN THE MANAGERS' meeting with Don, Kerry, Sarah, and Francoise, I say that, although the situation is dire, we may have a way to save the business. My thought is that we have a huge sale and try to sell off enough merchandise to buy out David. I tell them that, if we do this, we will probably have to sell so much, and at such a discount, that our inventory will be decimated, we will have cannibalized our future business, and we will have to move. It will be a daunting task. Francoise does not miss a beat. She says not to worry about it; we can always buy more. Sarah says that she realizes how much work this will be, but she thinks it is worth it. Kerry agrees. Don remembers how much work it was to move from our old location seventeen years ago. He figures that this will be harder because we have so much more merchandise, but he says that he is up for it. They are all so enthusiastic. I can't believe it. This will be incredibly hard, and it will be hardest on them. They all say that they believe we can make it work, and that they are more than willing to do what it will take.

I go to Bob and Tonia's for dinner. Setting foot in their house improves my mood dramatically every time I do it. They had a local architect design the house around their collections of antique Native American rugs and pottery, Mexican silver, *retablos,* and anything else that has caught their eye over the years. We dine at their seventeenth-century Spanish table and adjourn for brandy to my favorite room in the house, the domed library. I know they must be very curious about what is going on with Edish, but they are so kind and well-bred that they never ask. And I am so thrilled to not be talking about it for a few hours that I never bring it up either.

February 5, 2009

Ken and I have coffee early and discuss making an offer to have a huge sale in order to raise cash to pay off debts and buy out David. He wants me to pitch it to David, which I agree to do. I call my kids and sainted husband (it is not easy to get two six-year-olds dressed and fed, and make lunches, and still get to work on time without your shirt on backwards). Bruce does not like this plan at all. His worry is that we will put ourselves in the situation of overpaying for a business that will basically be a shell when we are done with our giant sale—not to mention that, thus far, even our best sales have not generated much business. Since he is my dear husband and closest advisor, I ignore his advice.

AT MY MEETING with David, I suggest that we have the big sale to buy him out. His lips tighten. He says absolutely not. We cannot raise money from a business he owns. We would have to give him his share of any money we raise. This is technically true, I tell him, but I am pretty sure it is

what the Harts did to buy out the Kays at the Antique Pavilion, and that, if he agrees to it, he would
have a bunch of cash and the employees could keep
their jobs. He is clear that there is no way that he
will consent.

Ken and I meet for lunch. We talk over various
options. We could, for example, borrow money to
buy David out. But no one is lending money right
now. And it might be slightly difficult, in this or
any environment, to convince someone to lend us
a huge chunk of money to overpay for a third of a
business that has a fair load of debt and is not profitable.

There is the possibility of *forcing* David to continue. I owe him some money, and he could call in
my shares against it (which would be great because
I wouldn't owe him the money any more), but then
he would own more than a third of the company.
Since he would not get all of my shares, Ken and I
would between us still own the majority of the
company. Although we could do it, neither one of
us has the stomach to put ourselves in the situation
of being in business with someone who does not
want to be in business with us, especially when
Edish is so financially precarious.

Ken and I sit there and don't look at each other
while we basically admit that we cannot figure out
a way to save Edish. I do not cry. I do not throw

up. I do feel like doing both.

Back at the shop, I look at the people whose hopes I got up yesterday, who volunteered to make their lives a living hell to make this business work, and know that I have to tell them as soon as I can. Don and I walk outside, and I tell him. Telling Kerry, Sarah, and Francoise next, each separately, is dreadful. Each one of them tells me that they will stay to the end and do anything they can to help. I am waiting for someone to scream or yell or list all the ways I have screwed up. It would be fair, and it would be true. They are each losing a job they have given everything to, in a terrible economy. None of them talks about that. They are, to a person, incredibly gracious.

Of all weird things, Jamario has been saving a bottle of champagne from the Antique Pavilion Christmas party in our little fridge. He wants to drink it while I'm here. We all stand around drinking champagne. I toast to Obama's election and Aretha's hat—the only two things I can think of to be cheerful about. What an awkward feeling to be looking at everyone and drinking champagne. I know I will have to tell the rest of the employees tomorrow morning. Being brave and tough, I get the hell out of there. Don walks me out and says, "Now I know what it felt like to be on the *Titanic*."

I go to Ken's and prepare to meet with David

and Ken.

The three of us sit down. David loves to hear the sound of his own voice and so starts to pontificate. We usually let him go on until we can't stand it anymore, but tonight I am not feeling that generous. I interrupt him and say, "We are going to end it." He wants to repeat how we arrived at this decision and why it is the best one. I say that we have agreed to do what he wants, that I will tell the employees tomorrow, and that we don't have much more to discuss tonight.

DAVID STARTS TO cry. Ken and I try not to look at each other. David looks at Ken and says through his tears, "I know you think I have no heart, but it is not true." Ken doesn't say a word; he gets up and walks away, leaving me sitting alone with David. Can I sue for that? Apparently he had to go to Siberia to get tissues, but he finally returns. David wants to talk more, to have us make him feel okay about all of this. I am usually the first to participate in that kind of thing, but I feel so angry and sad all at once that I don't. I say that I have to go, that I have dinner plans. Which I do. Ken says he has to go, too. David says that he would like to come to the meeting to tell the staff tomorrow, so he can "help" me. Finally, he leaves. In the meantime, Gary has come home. He graciously listens as I bitch about David crying about closing a business that he is basically forcing us to close. Maybe I am the one with no heart.

Leonard and Dave are having a party. I arrive about half an hour late. Don and Chelby, who will be late for their own funerals, beat me there and are drinking Veuve Clicquot out of Baccarat. Leonard starts to get me a glass, because who wouldn't want that? I rudely ask if I can have a martini instead. And fast. As I've already said, Leonard is the kind of friend I can behave this way with. He obliges. As all of us sit and talk, I think about how lucky I am to have these friends who will love me no matter how big of a failure I am.

When we first started talking about the possibility of closing Edish, David, Ken, and I agreed not to tell anyone, for a variety of reasons. Since I have told the managers and am going to tell everyone else tomorrow, I figure it is okay to tell Leonard. I brace myself, thinking of his past connections to Edish and how much he cares about so many people that work there. I lean in, martini in hand, to gently break it to him.

His response? That he has known for ages, because he works part time for David, who has been working with his staff for months to prepare them to go back into the china business as soon as Edish closes.

I feel my whole body get hot; I know that I am

flushed. The room spins. Leonard immediately backtracks and apologizes. He has nothing to apologize for. David's words of a couple of days ago about how he would never go back into the china business, or profit from Edish's demise ring, in my ears. I do everything I can to pull myself together and be a good party guest for the rest of the evening. I don't remember much, but I am sure I was charming and the life of the party.

Ken is asleep when I get home. I wish I were. Ambien is useless. As I lie in bed, I notice that my skin is literally hot to the touch. For the first time in my life, I understand the term *boiling mad*.

February 6, 2009

From 3 a.m. to 6 a.m., I wait to see a light from downstairs letting me know that Ken is up. He, like me, often doesn't sleep. When I finally see it, I follow him out in my pajamas to get the paper. When I tell him, he is furious. We plot revenge. I remind him about the first time I met Martha Stewart. She was telling someone that there is a kind of animal pee that you can leave on a person's doorstep that will make their house smell so bad they have to move. She was just kidding. Too bad.

THE MEETING WITH the employees is awful. David's presence exacerbates it. I'm sure it doesn't help that I can hardly look at him. I tell everyone that we are closing, that we think it will be May 31. That we hope they can all stay that long or as long as it takes, but that, of course, if they get a job opportunity they need to take it. I assure everyone that I will give them a great job reference, and that, in the meantime, if they need time off for interviews, we will always be able to work it out. I apologize to everyone, because I am really sorry.

David gets up to talk. He cries. This elicits the deepest sympathy from me. Okay, maybe not. Then he goes on to tell these people, who have just heard that they are going to lose their jobs, how he, Ken, and I are losing gobs of money on this deal. After telling them what kind of attitude they should have about our closing (cheerful), he says that he will also give them good job references but only if they stay till the end.

Next, I ask to meet separately with each em-ployee. David announces that he is going to join me. They all tell me that they will stay to the end and do whatever it takes to help.

David tells Francoise that he will hire her when Edish is finished. He told me this a long time ago, and I was relieved. As a single mother, she had so much to lose. And she is so intense that, although she is an incredibly hard worker, I know it will be hard for her to find another job. Like most of us, her greatest gifts and her biggest flaws are wound tightly together. She gets more done than any three people I know, but she sometimes leaves scorched earth in her wake. She has developed much more self-confidence working for me as a china buyer than she ever had working with David as a dish scrubber. When he first told me that he would hire her if Edish didn't make it, I thought he was being generous and smart. Now, of course, it is clear that it is so much more than that. She can make his china business happen.

Don says that he really doesn't want to meet with David. To my deep regret, I push him to do it anyway. Don was David's first employee. Back then, David and I were friends. He told me that hiring Don was the smartest thing he had ever done. At the time, David told me that Don doubled his sales immediately. Don is so friendly and easy-going with customers, I'm sure it was true. Years ago, David told me a story about sending Don somewhere far away to pick up a bunch of china. On the way back, the van broke down. David said he worried all night about Don making it home safely. This, of course was before cell phones. We are all old. And we are far from those moments. Don has been so upset by the events of the past few days, I wish that I had never gotten his hopes up.

The meeting with the three of us is uncomfortable, but we get through it.

ONCE DAVID AND I have met with everyone, I stick around the shop so that anyone who wants to talk to me can. Instead of fireworks, everyone, to a person, is kind and caring towards me. Responding to losing their livelihood with kindness towards the person who failed them is over the top, but that is what each person does.

I am worn out from lack of sleep and swirling emotions. I ask Don if he wants to duck out with me. Neither of us is going to be useful today. Plus, what is going to happen if we leave? We'll get fired? It is barely noon. We go to P.F. Chang's, sit at the bar, and drink and tell Edish stories. He tells me that, a few weeks ago, he showed up at the Antique Pavilion just as Wynonne was struggling to get the door unlocked. Her hands were full, so she said to him, "Here, hold my hair," and handed him the big blond ponytail that usually sits atop her head. It never would have occurred to me that it wasn't real.

I tell him about the guy who called a few weeks ago to order china. When I asked for his email address, he said, "I am a real doctor."

"O.K.," I replied, thinking that his mother must be so proud. "May I please have your email address?"

"Penisdoctor@hisInternetprovider.com," he said in a flat voice.

DON SHARES WITH me his dream of opening a mid-century decorative arts museum in Houston called DADA. Decorative Art and Design Association will, of course, not be related to MOMA. He tells me the long version. It is so nice to talk about something positive and unrelated to Edish. He is sweet and thoughtful and puts his arm around me. We are both still in a state of shock, but I have a glimmer that life will go on.

Back at the Antique Pavilion, I tell Wynonne what has happened. She is very supportive. When I ask if we can stay after our lease is up (which is the end of March), she tells me that I can take as much time as I want. Her mission at the moment seems to be not to add to my troubles.

When I ask about her legal situation, she tells me that she thinks there is a good chance that they will get probation. I don't know much about it, but I wonder whether she is right. I ask how I can help; she asks me to write a letter to the judge. I can't imagine that he would care much about what I have to say, but of course I agree. She tells me that she will have her attorney contact me about the letter. When I ask her if she would like me to come back for her sentencing hearing, one of the toughest women I have ever gotten to know tears up and say that she would really appreciate it. She takes a big drag on yet another cigarette , and we say good bye.

February 7, 2009

I fly home. In Park City, there is a company that takes people on balloon rides. When I drive the kids to school in the mornings, we often see a balloon aloft, looking magical, like something straight out of *The Wizard of Oz*. Once it has descended and the passengers have left for other exciting adventures, the balloon lies on the ground, deflated, ready to be trucked away. I am that balloon.

February 9, 2009

Having asked the Houston employees not to tell anyone in Salt Lake that we are closing, I tell them myself. No one seems too shocked. Rebecca, in Houston, sends me an email asking how they took it and how I am doing. She is worried about me! When I tell her that they were wonderful, and that I am feeling sad and wishing I had done so many things differently, she replies: "I'm so sorry, Miriam. We all love you, and no one has anything bad to say about you. You can always be proud of what you have done at Edish." Unbelievable. Proud is not exacting what I am feeling.

Kerry forwards an email from a customer whose china he has just declined to buy. I think we all just want to pass along anything positive at this moment. She writes: *Hi Kerry, while I'm disappointed to hear that my china is not in demand, I do appreciate your speedy reply. I called last week and talked with a very friendly person. It's refreshing to find an Internet company that consists of real, nice people. Pat.*

We get feedback like this all the time. It seems a little bittersweet today. When I ask how Kerry is doing, he says that he is adjusting to the idea, and that he thinks he has the insurance thing figured out. He knows that I have been worried about this for him; I'm sure he can get a retail job, because he is so good at it. But we both know that, unlike Edish, most stores do not offer their sales people insurance. He goes on to say, "I feel bad that you feel bad. . . . Just don't spend a lot of time beating yourself up about this. You are not at fault in this, and if we have to look for somebody to blame a little bit, I guess it's the co-owner who never attended a store meeting until the company was going out of business. And there is no point in blaming anybody."

The kindness and generosity of a group of people who are about to lose their jobs is a bit overwhelming.

February 10, 2009

On the way to the airport, to drop off my mother, she wants to talk about what is going on. I know she is worried about me, but I just don't feel like blabbing about it, and, given everyone's response, it seems tacky to whine—which is what I feel like doing. So instead, I behave like a perfect angel with my mother. Or not. We always seem to have an argument on the way to the airport. I am getting a little long in the tooth to argue with my mother like an adolescent. After cooking and cleaning and buying my kids every article of clothing they could ever need, I should understand that, when she says, "You're wearing *that?*" or "You *can't* let your daughter go to the *grocery* store looking like *that!*" what she really means is that she loves me, and that that she has probably refrained from saying one hundred other rude but true things about my housekeeping or childrearing skills.

Chapter Four

"The most beautiful curve is a rising sales graph."[6] *—Raymond Loewy*

February 11, 2009

We start emailing our 220,000 customers this letter:

> After nearly twenty-five years in business, the last ten as Edish, we find that we must close our doors. We expect to be out of business by May.
>
> Starting today, we will offer a 35% discount on ALL merchandise. This may not be combined with any other sales or promotions and it does exclude prior sales. All items will be first-come, first-served.
>
> To our Customers: Over the years, many

of you have shared your lives and your stories with us. Many of you have known us and shopped with us for decades. Some of you have only learned about us recently. I want to thank all of you.

I would like to say a few words to acknowledge the Edish elves: At some point you have probably encountered Don, who started with us in 1988. . .or have sold china to Francoise, who started in 1989, or gotten an email from Kathi, our Database Manager (1990). Maybe Kerry has waited on you, but he has been with us a mere thirteen years. Craig and Bob and Rose have been doing this for ten years. Then there are the newbies like Sarah, Jamario, Aaron, Rebecca, Lindsey, Dale, and Jeremy, who have been with Edish for only five years or less. I am so fortunate to have been involved with the most hard-working, dedicated, caring people I have ever met. What an incredible group.

About the SALE: Over the next several months we will offer increasingly large discounts on our merchandise. All items will be first-come, first-served. There will be no holds or layaways. We will no longer be buying china, crystal, flatware, or gifts, so shop early for the best selection. Starting today all items that are not already on sale will be 35% off our already very low prices.

Of course, this may not be combined with other discounts and does exclude prior sales.

Our return policy will change. We will no longer be as lenient as we have been about the time period. Through the end of March, all items must be returned with original stickers within one week to qualify for a refund.

Although it is with great sadness that I send this email, I must also say that it has been a great thrill to have worked with our staff and with (most) of our customers. We have loved having you in our lives.

One final note: if you know of job opportunities that might be appropriate for any of the Edish elves, either in Salt Lake City or Houston, or beyond, please let me know.

According to our files you are interested in the following patterns:

February 12, 2009

What happens next is shocking. Keep in mind that we are offering a discount of 35%, and that in the last six months we have put virtually every pattern on sale at 30% off and gotten an utterly meager response.

"Stop sending emails about the sale!" Sarah begs. There are hundreds of orders from the website. We can't keep up. The phones are ringing off the hook. Both stores are mobbed with people. The floodgates are opened.

We stop sending emails.

But this is not the most amazing part. Hundreds of people respond to our letter. They either include a comment with their order or they just hit *reply*:

> *Dear people at Edish,*
>
> *I am so sorry to hear you are going out of business; it was always one of my favorite things to do to stop by and browse through your vast supply of goodies. Your service has always been outstanding, and the people who waited on me always helpful and polite and well-informed.*
>
> *Thanks for so many years of good dishes and glassware! I will miss stopping by.*
>
> *I've used your service for years. . .I'm heartbroken you are by far the best at providing my pattern at a reasonable price.*
>
> *It makes me so sad to lose you.*
>
> *I am so sorry to hear this! I love your store in Houston. My son came with me one time and swore to my husband that he had never seen me have such an estrogen rush. This is so sad.*

Thanks too for the memories!

Dear Edish good people,

I am so sad at the news I just received. You have been so good to us. I am a retired architect with a love of good design. When I was setting up my first apartment, I needed china and purchased a Thomas iteration of Raymond Loewy's Rhythm, white, undecorated. I did not know at the time that there was an earlier and finer version. Anyway, there were several breakages over the years, and I had too few pieces to serve a dinner party. My local sources didn't know Rhythm from Melmac, and then I found Edish online. Thanks to you I have the most impeccable china in the fine quality I always aspired to. For old times' sake I have just made a purchase online of some odds and ends. I feel that I am losing friends. Many many thanks, and my personal good wishes to all who made one of my many unfulfilled wishes get so happily filled. Bon appétit.

No, not you!

It is a shock to learn that you are closing the store. I spent so many hours wandering those aisles. . .I am saddened.

Thanks so much. I am sorry to hear you are closing. I know it's a hard decision. We closed our business after seventy-nine years last year. It's a tough call and I wish you all the best.

I was so sad to read your email. . .it is heart-breaking what is happening to our economy/country, and I wish all of you the best of luck in your new adventures.

I've been using your wonderful service since 1985, when I ordered a bunch of this pattern after I got married. So sad to hear you're closing your doors. Thanks for everything over the years.

I am so sorry to hear of your closing. It seems this is happening at so many places, including where my wife and I work. I hope all your people are blessed with a new career somewhere soon. Thanks for staying in touch through the years!

Sniff. . .sniff. . .cry. . . Luv your guts always!

None of us knew quite how to respond to this one:

Who can stop this domino effect? America is losing its free-enterprise system. Stores are

*closing, you are closing. There is no building of
cars, houses, or buildings. We are not working
on a highway or a transportation system. America needs to wake up and get something going.
We can't all sit on our butts and wait on a check.
The Mexicans have gone home to a country where
they cannot get a job or enough food. The world
is sinking. Can you try harder to stay in business?
I know the banks all got money, and they kept it
and gave the stockholders a dividend check and
the managers a bonus.*

This one, like so many of the letters we got, was
yet another reminder that so many people were in
the same boat:

Dear Miriam,

*Thank you for telling me. I share your sad-
ness since I had to close my business this month,
too. It was said to me that everyone who wants
to stay "vital" should look ahead, as if your best
work (no matter what it is) is yet to be.*

I do wish you the best in your next endeavor.
Best regards,

Dear Miriam,

*Thank you for the very kind thoughts about
the people who have helped your business these*

many years. I've probably only spent $50 with your store, but I feel richer for knowing the love and care that your group has shown each other.

I am sure that there are times that make you question what this all means, but I can only imagine the blessing you have given your business's team—food on all their tables, the vacations you helped provide. . . . I hope you get to step back and see how worthwhile it has all been. May God bless you as he leads you to the new adventures in your life.

Bless you, Miriam, for sending out such a nice letter. You have made dreams come true for so many people by finding and supplying meaningful items they thought were gone forever.

They treasured the items and you as well for the job you have done, and it's particularly nice to find out that you've been a great businesswoman and obviously a good boss that appreciated her staff.

As one businesswoman to another, I've been in the art business and owned and curated three galleries. That's all in the past now. So I know what it is like to close the door to what was once a labor of love. I wish you every happiness in all your future endeavors. Remember that, when one door closes, another opens. So may all the joy you *brought to others over the years return to you ten-fold. Bravo and good luck.*

I regret to hear what all you are going through, and I know this is a difficult decision you've made. I understand because, during the early 1970s, my husband and I owned one of the largest recreational vehicle dealerships in the south east. The second energy crunch came along, and what it didn't get us with during the first one it took everything we'd worked seventeen years to build up. We'd also built a new showroom with offices in the building, and a new shop building, about 1969. It was a beautiful operation with great people working for us, and we were doing good and ready for a long and profitable business. We had over a hundred people working in sales, office, shop, and accessory store. We worried so much about those families that were affected by what was going on in our business. Lucky for us, they all understood and knew what we had to do. Hard times come to all of us at some point in our lives, and I will tell you we survived, and after that was all settled we went to real estate school and did well. God will take care of you during this difficult and painful time. My prayers will be with all of you. Keep the Faith.

This came through from a regular customer of ours in Salt Lake City whom we had watched fight a heroic battle with cancer. Her first outing after being in the hospital, unable for months to walk, was to come shop at Edish. Craig had called her to let her know that we were going out of business.

> *I can't stand the thought of you not being there. I will miss coming into the store and most of all visits with you and Craig. I have been out of town and got home this morning. Tell Craig thanks for his call as I am not good about checking my email and so was glad to hear his message this morning.*
>
> *I will be by and maybe buy.*

Scores of people echoed the one-door-closing, another-opening sentiment.

These emails go on for weeks. We are buried in more orders than we can possibly handle.

February 23, 2009

We pay off Gary. Our debt to him had been almost six figures. This is an exciting day. We still have more back bills to pay off, including the huge postage bill, but we are moving in the right direction.

Don sends and email with the subject line *You are going to think I am crazy but...*

> *Edish is fun to work at right now even though it's really busy. I am finishing lunch, and I am looking forward to going out to the sales floor. People are buying the way they should have been. Customers are kind and thoughtful and engaging and appreciative and patient because they know we are closing. I have only seen one person try to get a better price, so there is no discomfort or time and energy wasted on negotiation. The staff is getting along more or less. There is little to no buying and identification activity contaminating the selling activity the way it always did. I can get rid of any salesperson who calls with ease! There are entirely new, fresh problems to worry about instead of making payroll and paying bills. Now staffing and supplies and managing orders are the concern as in a healthy business. Just thought you might like to hear a crazy perspective on the current state of our business.*

It is funny, but I feel the same way. Everyone is working so hard, but it is a little like Christmastime, when we are so busy but most customers are in a good mood and most of us are, too. Each of us is totally worn out at the end of the day, but no one seems to mind much.

People coming into the store are so nice, and customers keeps sending the most lovely and deeply personal emails:

> You are wonderful and I have enjoyed every dish that I have bought from you. My Mom died almost a year ago, and I entered your store more for free advice than purchase. The people in your store are very compassionate and kind.
>
> I will keep my ears open, and thanks for your love to customers. This note is just an example. You did more than sell stuff. You care and always will.

> For me, your firm makes it possible to purchase a tea set that I probably wouldn't otherwise have. Glamis Thistle is indelibly associated with my beloved great-aunt, a surrogate grandmother who was safe haven for me during unhappy childhood years amidst an emotionally cold and hypercritical family. I never thought I would see this china again. My aunt's china disappeared after she passed on, the excuse given that family assumed I wouldn't be interested in her old things.

> When I was told of an online auction, making it possible to buy a six-setting set with two serving plates, I was beside myself with joy. However, it

was making and serving of tea and luncheon with this set that brought me to your virtual doorstep in recent months, in search of a tea set.

Thus, almost thirty years later, I was able to set my old round oak table with antique linen and this beautiful china, to make a pot of this aunt's favorite tea, scones, and shortbread. In a haze of tears, I sat down to re-create memory of past happiness. The wash of deep satisfaction, a feeling of long-sought 'rightness,' settled in.

It felt like 'coming home.'

Yay and verily, Miriam. Thanks for the memories.

I don't want to sound like Pollyanna. Not everyone who was contacting us was so selfless. One of the things I didn't count on when asking people about job opportunities in my letter was that a significant portion of our customers live in Utah. Utah, as I learned after I moved here, has the highest per capita number of multi-level companies of any state. I had never even heard of "multi-level" before I moved here. I sell a product to you (at a party at my house, of all things) and get you to start selling it, and I get a percentage of everything you sell. At least I think that is how it works. I've been offered all kinds of things. My first was a laundry ball—a plastic ball that costs $75.00. You never have to use detergent again. Except that my mother was right—if it sounds too good to be true, it is. It turns out that most of us use too much detergent, so there is residual detergent on our clothes for the first few washes. After that, the laundry ball ceases to be effective. Good luck getting your seventy-five bucks back.

So we got a ton of letters offering multi-level-product, commission-only sales jobs. But for every one of those, we got ten letters like this one from one of the best bakeries in town:

> Miriam:
>
> What a shock to receive your email, and I read it with such sadness. You may not know me, but I have shopped there often. Our business was damaged during Ike, and we are hoping to get the permit soon to rebuild. Once we get closer to opening, we are going to be hiring people to work in our store in April and May. If any of your employees are interested, they can call me or email. I wish you and your employees all the best, and I am truly so very sad. I loved your place.
>
> Janice Jucker
> Three Brothers Bakery

Houstonians just say "Ike," and everyone knows what they mean. Last year hurricane Ike whipped through Houston, wreaking unbelievable havoc. Insurance on our inventory was out of our reach, so I was panicked when the hurricane was on its way; I stayed up all night at home in Utah, watching it on CNN. All I could do was observe the disaster unfold while thinking about how much money we owed Gary, and if we would be able to pay it back if our shop was destroyed. . .what everyone would do for a job. . .all kinds of cheery thoughts.

There was plenty of notice, so many of the employees had evacuated, which in and of itself was a nightmare. Francoise called me frantically to say that she was trying to get to Dallas, but that there was no gas to be found. Finally, she found an open gas station and waited hours but at least was able to fill up. It took her and her daughter seventeen hours to get to Dallas, usually a five-hour drive. Don and Chelby stayed put, because they have a mid-century house that floods. I thought they were crazy and begged them to leave.

Hurricane Katrina was on all of our minds. I told everyone to make sure they had my home phone number and address, and that, if it was bad, to just make it to my house. That, of course, was ridiculous. It is a day-and-a-half drive on a clear day and a half. I was terrified and totally helpless.

Edish was relatively unscathed. The Antique Pavilion had some damage to the outside, but Jack and Cathy (this was before "the coup") had done a great job of boarding up everything, so none of the picture windows were broken. Kerry lives across the street, so I called him hourly for updates. Miraculously, Edish still had power. Most employees, and hundreds of thousands of other people in the area, went without power for weeks.

Non-essential employees were supposed to stay home for several days. Edish people do not consider themselves non-essential. In spite of the fact that I told everyone to take as long as they needed, virtually all of them were ready to come back in a couple of days. Giant trees in the street, no electricity, flooded homes, and general destruction that looks like the apocalypse do not engender big spending on china and crystal. We did virtually no business in Houston for weeks. I say "virtually" because one of our oldest and dearest customers came in shortly after the hurricane and made a big pile of things to buy on our front counter. Looking Don in the eye, she said, "I came in 'cause I knew y'all would need the business." It takes a lot to make Don teary-eyed.

THANKS TO GARY, we were able to borrow more money. Ike definitely helped us to dig ourselves into a much deeper hole than ever before, which of course put us in such a rocky position the following year when the economy tanked. So, yes, I had a lot of compassion for Janice Jucker of Three Brothers Bakery.

Because money was so tight, Francoise asked the one company that we wholesaled dishes to, Replacements, Ltd, to expedite payment to us. Every three months they publish a huge book, thicker than the New York City phone book, with tiny print, indicating what they will pay for millions of pieces of discontinued china. Francoise, Lindsey, Craig, Kerry, and I would split up a list of our inventory and comb through the book to see what we could sell to them. We would ship them things and get paid three or four weeks later.

After Ike, when it seemed like we were going to go under, we got much more aggressive about what we would send them. And Francoise called and asked if they could process our things faster and get us the money quicker than usual. They were incredibly helpful and got us our money in record time. It was one of the things that saved us. This was all the more remarkable because we were their competition—not much, though, considering that they were selling more than thirty-five times what we were, but still.

When things settled down, I wrote the CEO a thank-you note for helping us through that troubled time. Of all things, he sent me a check, made out to me personally for $200.00. I was floored. And a little embarrassed. I called him to thank him and to tell him that I couldn't accept it. It wasn't as if I couldn't put food on the table.

March 3, 2009

Incredibly, we are still going gangbusters. Don emails yet again what several of us are thinking:

> I think you would be amazed if you were down here to look at it. It's one thing to see the numbers. . .it's quite another to see the shop full of people, the stacks of unprocessed sales, every surface available including temporary tables, empty stockroom shelves and, carts filled with orders. A wall of a hundred packages is pretty impressive, too.
>
> The general feeling of those who observe and participate has gone to beyond being shocked and sad that we are going out of business, to include that we must be idiots to close if we are this busy and it won't let up.

When I agree, he replies:

> There is no 35%-off sale that would have had this impact. . .except a going-out-of-business sale. So how do you harness the buying potential of our customers without doing this? Aaaarrrrrgh! We

tried for years!

We have always had an amazing inventory and customer base. The problem must have been perception. The inventory must have had the appearance of a stable commodity that would be available to a customer when she got good and ready to buy. Now, they know it's not going to be there anymore and it's 35% off. People feel a sense of urgency and competition. This has been a hell of a chance to see the psychological and sociological factors in economics.

Yes, it has.

March 6, 2009

We are all starting to feel we can breathe again. Having been working at breakneck speed for too many days in a row, each of us is cranky. Craig sends me a pissy email about the personal hygiene of the people he works with. Sarah and Rebecca have an argument. Everybody is mad at someone.

People inquire about buying our mailing list or website or business. I have several long conversations with people who, it turns out, have no money to buy it, or no idea what running a business this size entails, or who are like *this* guy. We have done some business with him in the past, but everyone fights over who has to help him because he is super-high maintenance; he emails:

> *We have bought and sold to you in the past, and we are sorry to hear that you will be closing your doors soon and would like to wish you and your employees best of luck in your future endeavors. We have interest in possibly purchasing a large quantity of stock as well as data and customer information. Is it possible for me to give you a call and discuss this further? If you provide me with a number and time, I'll be glad to follow up, or you can call me during regular business hours. I'm looking forward to hearing from you at your earliest convenience.*

What I should have said was, "I'm too busy. I'll call you in a year."

Of course I called. Twice. Two forty-minute conversations with him picking my brain about how to succeed in this business. (Perhaps the joke is on him after all. . .would you have asked me for advice on this topic?) The whole time we talked, he acted as if he was very interested in buying a big chunk of our business. At that point in my life, forty minutes times two was a considerable outlay of time.

At the end of the second conversation, he told me that he would have to borrow the money to make a substantial purchase like this, and he didn't think he could do that.

Hadn't he known that eighty minutes before?

ALL OF US are all feeling the strain. Feeling irritable and snappish seems unfair with this vast outpouring of support. People come into both stores, wanting to talk about why we are going out of business. We are just trying to get through the day. I guess it is like when someone dies. People feel they should say something, but it is hard to know what. Many well-wishers just say that they are sorry, which works pretty well. The employees all struggle with what to say when people want more details. They want to be polite, but they are tired and cranky and have answered the same questions ten times in one day. I tell one person, "Because you didn't shop here enough." For some weird reason, that cheers all of us up.

March 9, 2009

Wynonne calls the shop, my home, and my cell, looking for me. She is nothing if not persistent. It is not about the rent, because we paid it in full on the first. This is big news. For years, we had been paying half on the first and half on the fifteenth; paying all at once feels like a major victory.

I wonder if there is news about her case. She should be focusing all of her energy on trying to stay out of jail.

When I return her urgent call, it is not about her problems but mine. She has heard David talking about going to 50% off right away. She presses me hard not to do that. I tell her about our huge response to 35%. Her reply is that she is quite aware of the response, because the store is packed. How many customers do we have? she asks. I tell her 220,000. How many sales have we had since we sent the email? I have no idea, but I guess a couple thousand, maybe more. It feels like a million. She yells into the phone, in her smoky voice, "That is a less than 5% response! How many emails do you get that you ignore?"

This woman is smart. She reminds me that David's motivation is to get the business closed ASAP, but that even *he* should want to maximize our return. Telling me that he has "informed" her that he will be renting our space when we move out, she says that her response was to inform him that it was not his decision.

Sending out another email about continuing our 35%-off sale had not occurred to me. It proved to be a hard sell with David. But she was right. Having just liquidated their huge auction house/antique gallery the previous year, she had become an expert at going out of business. She was giving me the benefit of everything she learned by hiring an expensive firm to run their closing sale. Unbelievably, she was worrying about me when she had her own, much larger problem looming on the horizon. Luckily for us, she took the time to track me down and pound her ideas into me.

Chapter Five

*"I find it harder and harder every
day to live up to my blue china."*[7]
—Oscar Wilde

March 10, 2009

A woman who used to be our shipper several
years ago comes into the Houston store to say
hello. She is a hard worker, but her life has always included some huge drama or other. At the
time she worked for us, we had a policy of drug-
testing anyone who had an accident at work. My
opinion has always been that what you do in your
free time is none of my damn business, but what
you do at work is. The test came back positive
for some serious drugs, and we had to let her go.
Several years have passed; told she looks great

and is sober, I have Don ask her if she would like
to come back and help us part time. Jamario and
Leonard (who is helping us part time when he is
not working for David) are buried in shipping.
Hard work is this woman's specialty.

March 11, 2009

Don emails me:

> Every once in a while, you can go back and
> change an ending from a long time ago. I think it
> has to be pretty rare though. Giving V. a chance
> was a very nice thing for her and for Edish. That
> was your call, and it was a good one.
>
> She won't stop thanking us for the second
> chance, and she rocked when she was here on the
> weekend. When we discussed her pay today, she
> said she would work for free just for getting the
> second chance. She was about to cry, and I was
> so touched I gave her $12 instead of $11.85, which
> she made when she left!!
>
> She is crazy. . .like a fox!

My reply:

> Do you know how many martinis we could
> buy with that 15 cents? Or how much scotch tape
> David could buy?

Don says:

> *I know. I figured if she works a hundred hours between now and the time we close, that would be fifteen bucks. . . enough for a martini for you and me to split, and two rolls of scotch tape for David!*

Ugh. On top of everything else, I tell my Salt Lake City landlord that we will be moving out at the end of May, when our lease is up. His response is to tell me that our lease is not up until May of next year. I feel my face getting hot and turning red. I am furious that he would pull something like this. He goes on to tell me that there is no way he can lease the building in this economy. He does not mention the fact that the roof leaks, the plumbing doesn't work right, and the building is falling apart. After he leaves, I go to my file cabinet and realize that he is right. Oops.

I wonder how I will be able to tell Ken and David.

Deciding to face my problems head on, I email Ken:

> *I need to tell you about a mistake I made. It is a big deal, and I am dreading telling you. I am doing it via email because I am a wimp.*
>
> *I was wrong about our Salt Lake City lease.*

It is not up until the end of May of next year. I am really sorry. I feel like an idiot, and I don't know how I could've misread it. I remember trying to look at the file quickly at the store because I was afraid it would be obvious to the employees that we were thinking about closing the store. But that is not an excuse.

Our landlord doesn't want to let us out of the lease. I am going to see if I can lease it myself. If I can find someone, I'll see if he will transfer the lease to them because I don't want the liability.

I am very very sorry.

Ken, Mr. Difficult, responds:

You are handling the big issue of closing down a business after years, and this is what got you down? Chin up, my sweet.

I might not be good at picking a business. . .but I do okay in the friend department.

March 16, 2009

Several months ago, Don and I were both interviewed for an article in *Martha Stewart Living*. Today we receive an email from a customer:

Dear Edish,

I just read about your wonderful site in the brand new copy of Martha Stewart Living. *I am hoping all the new interest might save you.*

Neither one of us even has time to go buy the magazine and read the article. How things have changed.

Years ago, I wrote Martha a letter. It was a little cheeky. Two days later, her assistant, Ann E. Armstrong (who later figured heavily in Martha's legal issues), called and said, "Martha would love to meet you." I thought it was one of my employees playing a joke.

We set up a time, and I did everything I could to prepare for the meeting. The employees in the Salt Lake store knew about the meeting, as did Don and Ken and my family, and that was it. I wasn't sure how it would go, but I didn't want anyone getting in the middle and messing it up.

Everyone who knew had advice for me. The most shocking came from my mother and grandmother, who for the first time in my life said, "Whatever you do, don't wear a dress. Martha wore pants to the White House."

As an aside, a very strange thing happened to me on the plane to New York. As I have said, I like my private time on planes.

About halfway through the flight, a young woman across the aisle asked me if I would like to read her magazine. I was so fidgety she probably just wanted to calm me down.

She asked me why I was going to New York, and for some reason I told her. Her eyes got really big. She went on tell me that she was a stock analyst for Martha Stewart Omnimedia. Shocked as I was, there was more. She and her boss, she said, met with Martha quarterly. Prepping me for my meeting became her mission for the rest of the flight. Virtually everything she told me would happen did. If I hadn't met her, I would not have been prepared for any of it, and I would not even have gotten to meet with Martha Stewart.

AN HOUR BEFORE the meeting, Ann E. Armstrong called to cancel. The woman on the airplane had told me that this would happen. Martha's stock numbers were coming out that day, and she said Martha would be swamped. I asked whether Martha was still in Manhattan. She said, "Yes, why?"

I told her that I had flown to New York for this meeting, was really looking forward to it, and could meet Martha anywhere in town, even if it was just for a few minutes. Armstrong, who was incredibly sweet in every interaction I had with her, not at all a black-clad famous-New-York-person's-assistant type, giggled. She told me that I was persistent, a trait she knew Martha appreciated, and that she would see what she could do, but she was not hopeful.

When she called me back she said, "Be at the office in two hours."

I was. As the woman on the airplane had promised, I was offered water or Diet Coke. She'd told me, "Whatever you do, do not ask for regular Coke." I didn't. I may not be smart, but I know how to follow instructions.

Martha came in with the then-editor of her magazine. Tall, beautiful, and confident, she really is larger than life. She was in the middle of the story about someone she was angry with, saying the thing about the animal-pee product you could leave on a person's doorstep that would smell so bad that they would have to move. The magazine editor was mortified that she was talking this way in front of me. Martha said, "Oh, Miriam knows I'm just kidding." I did. But it occurred to me that it might be a good idea not to make this woman angry.

There were some flowers on the table; she called someone to come up and look at one of the colors in one of the flowers, and she said, "I want that color in my paint collection." Poof, another Martha Stewart paint color was born. This is not a woman who kibitzes. Everyone else left, and we sat down to talk about Edish and look at the website. She was remarkably well informed about the discontinued china business. I think she was also aware of the impact that she had on the market, but I told her anyway.

There are lots of examples, but the most obvious was Jadeite, a green kitchen glass from the 1930s and '40s that we used to not even bother to try to sell. We couldn't give it away. Then Martha started collecting it and talking about it on her TV show. Once she did that, of course, we could offer it at practically any price, and we'd sell out. Almost everything she collected was like that.

I started to show this woman with a (well-deserved) reputation for perfection my website. So of course it crashed. I wished a giant chasm would open in the floor and swallow me whole.

I could get nothing to show up on that screen but a big black *Page Unable To Load 401 Error*. Although, I expected her to declare the meeting over, Martha told me not to worry about it; she had already looked at our site and loved it. We talked for an hour. Armstrong walked me out. She was very encouraging.

Within a couple of weeks her staff contacted me to ask me to be on her TV show. They were an intense group of people. Every single thing had to be perfect. They told me what to wear (a solid color, but not the one Martha would be wearing). A seven-minute segment took months of work. I wrote a script. They revised it. And revised it. I sent them boxes and boxes of china and crystal to use on the show. The week before the taping, Martha looked at it and decided she didn't like most of it, and I sent tons more. And rewrote the script. Then the staff rewrote it. It was about the discontinued china business and how to sell your china. It was like a giant commercial for Edish. The staff told me that it was my job to bring Martha back to the script when (not if) she strayed. That seemed likely.

I flew to the East Coast, where my mother spent two days taking me to every store in the universe to find a solid color outfit. Then I went to the TV studio in Westport, Connecticut. Andy Warhol famously said that, in the future, everyone would have fifteen minutes of fame. I only had seven, but it was still pretty cool.

Her staff got me ready; then Martha arrived. We shot the segment. Seven minutes seems like a long time if you are writing a script, but when you are filming it, if you blink you miss it. Although she was obviously in a hurry, she was very friendly. She joked around with me and with the cameraman and, when the shooting was over, asked me if I wanted a cappuccino. Realizing that this was going to my only chance to have coffee with a famous person, I said yes. She waved her hand and, like magic, one appeared. And she was gone. You don't shoot an hour show five days a week in seven minute segments by sitting around with me. I was flabbergasted with how congenial she had been to me, and about Edish.

Speaking of website crashes, we had some spectacular ones when the segment aired. The response was wild. Every time they re-aired it, we had terrific business.

Over the years there have been rumblings about Martha's behavior with business associates. I can only speak for myself. She was very gracious to me. I hardly expected her, a busy woman with what can only be called an empire to run, to be my buddy.

This is not exactly an original thought, but it always struck me that if a man running a huge company behaves like that, he is smart and efficient. If a woman does, she's a bitch.

But what do I know?

March 17, 2009

I email Don that the Martha Stewart article must have come out and that at least we are going out with a bang. His reply: *Right. Bang, bang, we're dead.*

March 18, 2009

It is time to focus on someone else's problems for a change. Wynonne's attorney sends an email describing what they have pled guilty to—misapplication of fiduciary funds. The attorney says that this is basically using funds from things that had been consigned to them, and then auctioned, to pay other bills. She goes on to say that, because they have never had any other trouble with the law, they are eligible, and hoping, for probation.

Having no connection to their legal issues, I can't speak to them, but I do write a letter for Wynonne about how kind she has been to me and how I hope she does not go to jail. When I speak to her, she sounds hopeful. She tells me that about 150 people are writing letters, including a former federal prosecutor and lots of well-known Houstonians.

When I tell her to hang in there and that I will see her in April for the trial, she again pushes me not to go to 50% off yet. She knows we can make more money if we do another round of 35%. Again, I marvel at her ability to worry about my problems instead of hers.

March 19, 2009

For some reason, today, mixed in with the rest of the customer's emails, were kind emails from two people who used to sell us china, and one from an old employee (the former butcher). Nice people coming out of the woodwork.

March 20, 2009

Positive feedback was especially welcome because of our next problem. Today we figure out why companies have been blocking us as spammers. This is a huge issue for us, and it has occurred a couple of times over the years. Typically it happens because we send out a lot of emails, so companies like Comcast or AOL think we are spammers. They then refuse to send out our emails. We only email people who have asked us to let them know about their patterns, but I guess if there is a lot of traffic coming from one place, the ISPs assume it is coming from an illegitimate source.

Also, lots of people forget that they signed up with us and report us as spammers. This happened well before computers, too. When we used little three-by-five-inch cards to write down people's info, we would call them when their pattern came in. Once a week, someone would freak out and ask how we got their number. Don used to say, "Yeah, we snuck into your house to see what your china pattern was, wrote it down, and called you when we found some more." Usually he said that after he hung up the phone. But not always.

The problem is that, once a big company decides that we are spammers, it is hard to get them
to change their minds. AOL once blocked us for
nearly a month. It almost put us out of business.
We couldn't contact our AOL customers via email.
They only relented when our congressman's office
got involved, when I pointed out to them that AOL
started blocking us *after* we stopped advertising
with them. It is shocking how much power Internet providers have.

In this instance someone hijacked our Edish-
gram email address. Ken had this set up so that, if
someone found a pattern they wanted to let someone else know about, they could send an Edish-
gram. It was cute, and it worked, and now someone
named hievoninchy@yahoo.com in the Philippines
hijacked it and was using it to send 5,500 spam
emails. Comcast wouldn't send any of our emails
out. Because this is what we most need in our lives,
Ken and Kathi work tirelessly to get the issue re-
solved. They eventually do.

March 23, 2009

Lindsey can't come to work because he has another kidney infection, which his doctor says can be
brought on by stress. What stress? You are working
like crazy at a job you are about to lose. Wimp.

March 24, 2009

Sarah starts to lose it and sends this email to a bunch of people in Houston:

> *I know everyone thinks I'm overreacting, but when there is an e-mail titled* Subject: Fw: Incorrect Billing Address On Internet Purchase, *I think someone should look at it. Someone worked around it to take care of websales, so it wasn't something that came in at the last minute.*
>
> *When I try to tell others about it, and am told, 'Well, I do not know what my role is on the sales floor. If you want me to do things like that on your day off, you should tell me. You should leave instructions for people to handle things when you aren't here. You should have someone assigned to handle things like this when you aren't here. Have you told X., Y., and Z.?', then, yeah, I'm going to get a little pissed off and start snapping.*
>
> *It wasn't pointing the finger at any one person. I'd already talked to Rebecca about it, knowing that she had left early, to remind her that e-mails need to be checked even though they aren't websales. I was trying to remind everyone and got treated like it was my fault because I dared to take a day off. It's not the first time in the last six weeks it's happened either. I should not have to have everyone together in one group to remind people that other*

things besides websales come in to the sales floor e-mail account, and that some of those things are problems directly relating to a websale!

I appreciate that everyone worked their ass off on Saturday being a man down and didn't call me once! I appreciate that people are trying to make an effort to be here on time, and are working on their days off.

Sarah

It is wonder we don't *all* have a kidney infection. We all need a week in Hawaii.

March 25, 2009

Instead, the Salt Lake City store Internet goes dead. We cannot do any work, including sales or shipping, without the computer. This is a sad state of affairs. I remember when we used to write up sales, in a little receipt book that we bought from the office supply store, with an old-fashioned implement called a pen. Our cash register was a worn-out cigar box. And now we are paralyzed because the Internet is down. I literally spend over four hours on the phone with someone from our phone company, asking for help, trying everything, and repeatedly asking if perhaps the Internet in our neighborhood is down. The nice young man tells me that there is no way that is the problem. Jeremy goes to their office an hour away to get a new modem. We hook it up. Still no Internet.

March 26, 2009

Surprise. The problem was that the Internet *was* down in our neighborhood. At least it is fixed. Who do I see about getting four hours of my life back? Don't have time for that; I have to write the next letter to our customers. Don and I work on it. He has been reading all of the lovely responses to our emails. He says, "I feel like we are hearing a fellow American who is god-fearing and self-aware tell their secret story with the tragic beginning and a heroic ending that makes us feel like life is worth living! It's like you're the President of the U.S., not just Edish!"

Okay, it is overblown, but I could use some encouragement today.

The email has the subject *The Way We Were*:

> It has been overwhelming that hundreds of you have taken the time to send us such personal emails in response to our announcement that we are going out of business. Thank you so much for your stories, your kind wishes, your job suggestions, your reminder that as one door closes another opens.
>
> As one of you wrote: "Know that your firm will live on in the hearts of your customers, who have found additional service pieces, replaced bro-

ken china, or purchased a set for themselves or someone else. We are the type that cherishes our china for its power to anchor us to healthy patterns of living, respectfully sharing well-prepared food without distraction, in the company of friends and family."

There were hundreds of people who wrote to tell stories of their interactions with Edish elves or about how happy they were when they received their long-lost china.

It is now time for us to move to a 50% discount. All items in our stores and on our website are now 50% off our original low prices.

We have all been moved by your kind and thoughtful response.

Thank you.

Yet again we got hundreds of incredibly wonderful emails.

March 27, 2009

Wynonne asks through the grapevine if we can pay our rent early. It is very exciting to have Don take her over a check. Too bad we had to be going out of business to have great cash flow.

March 30, 2009

Wynonne calls to say that she was blown away

by our giving her the check early. And that she is quite upset because Sarah has put yellow computer-generated signs up saying 50% *Off* all around the shop. Yellow is Edish's color. Apparently it is tacky. I tell Wynonne that Sarah will change them to white signs. In her spare time.

April 1, 2009

The Obamas meet with the Queen of England. The president gives the Queen an iPod. I mention this only because of what happens on April 8.

April 2, 2009

We are back to breakneck speed. And more stress. Good thing we are tough. And we keep getting comments like this:

> *Hate to see you go. What am I going to get my wife for gifts now?*

> *I've been damaged by your demise, weeping in Oregon.*

> *Best wishes to all. Elves, like cats, always land on their feet.*

And:

> Long-time customer. Thank you for your
> years of wonderful service and caring about pre-
> cious relics from the past like me!

It helps.

April 6, 2009

Cathy Kay emails me about some negative
press the Harts have gotten. It is an article from a
broadcast on Channel 39 in Houston by a local re-
porter named Dennis Spellman:

> There is nothing left but an empty lot where
> Hart Galleries used to be located on South Voss
> Road in Houston.
>
> The auction company has now filed for bank-
> ruptcy. The husband and wife owners, Jerry and
> Wynonne Hart, have pleaded guilty to first de-
> gree felonies, "misapplication of fiduciary prop-
> erty over 200 thousand dollars."
>
> "He's leading a fake life, a double life," said for-
> mer customer John Benoit, speaking of Mr. Hart.
>
> Benoit, his wife Laurie, and many others say
> the Harts have auctioned their property and not
> given them the money that's owed to them.
>
> The Benoits showed us photos of antiques
> they auctioned through Hart Galleries. They
> claim they either did not get the money that was

owed to them, or the property was auctioned at a lower price than they agreed to.

Jerry Hart would not go on camera but did tell us he owes the Benoits less than $21. Laurie Benoit says she's owed about $70,000. "He's either believing his own lies or just trying to keep up with them," said Laurie Benoit.

Jerry Hart denies he did anything wrong in his dealings with the Benoits, but he and his wife did plead guilty to a first-degree felony in their dealings with other customers.

Hart Galleries was established in 1938. On April 28, the Harts will be sentenced in Harris County. The Benoits say they just don't want anyone else to be victimized. "Don't let him get in business and steal from anybody else," said Laurie Benoit.

The Harts are expected to ask the Judge for probation.

This sort of thing is not likely to be helpful in their quest for said probation.

April 8, 2009

A customer writes:

It is sad to think that this is probably the last shipment I'll have, from you. It arrived quickly

*and in perfect condition. If it has 'moderate
wear,' I would still give it to the Queen instead
of an iPod! I can't see anything to fault, as usual
with your years of service.*

Business continues to be wild. Everyone is exhausted, even by the well-wishers. Surely it is some kind of psychological phenomenon, but the people who come in to the store day after day telling us how sorry they are that we are going out of business, and wanting to hear the story of why, are wearing us out. Not to say that everyone doesn't appreciate them much more than those who say, "Fifty percent off? Can you do any better?" The first time I heard Lindsey say, "Oh, you want the vulture discount?" I was taken aback by the rudeness of it. His response was to point out to me that perhaps I should be taken aback by the people who were asking for more than half off. We are all getting punchy.

April 10, 2009

Someone who places an order writes:

*In the Rock band world, we host Farewell
Tours year after year. . .maybe you could do that!*

I love this idea. Maybe I should get a sequined one-piece outfit.

Chapter Six

*"My life is based on the playful
search for beauty."* [8] —Eva Zeisel

April 11, 2009

Our neighbors Staci and Tony have a house
boat on Lake Powell. We are all going for a week.
Ken, Gary, my father and stepmother, Staci, Tony,
their daughter and her boyfriend, and my husband
and kids and I. Ken and Gary fly into Page, Ari-
zona; the rest of us drive down there in a caravan.
It is about a five-hour drive. Once we pick up Ken
and Gary and groceries for a week (groceries and
liquor for a week for twelve people is an awesome
sight, six shopping carts piled high), we get on the
boat. Normal people go to Lake Powell in the summer, when it is crazy hot and the water slide off the

back of the boat into the lake is wonderfully re-freshing. I picked this week because the kids were out of school. The water temperature is slightly higher than the ice cubes in our drinks. It even snows one day.

Of course, this is the day my father decides to show off his spear-fishing skills. He brought a bow with a yellow arrow to "catch" fish. He set it up, saw a fish, pulled back the arrow and shot. The arrow missed the fish. Good thing, since he had forgotten to attach it to the bow. The arrow is now seven or eight feet under water that is just barely warmer than the polar ice cap. He says he will put his bathing suit on and get it. Hoping to cement my status as his favorite, I insist on going after it instead. After putting on my suit, I dive after the arrow. My heart constricts as I come up with no arrow, unable to breathe; I have never experienced anything like it. In his "dad" voice, he says, "I'll do it." Knowing how far we are from medical help and unsure whether I am in his will, I insist that I can go back under and get it. I do. As I shiver, back on the boat, Staci points out that the arrow proba-bly cost less than five dollars. I inherited my brains from my father.

The great news is that there is no cell or Inter-net service out here, and that the only person less interested in talking about Edish than I am is Ken.

So in spite of the fact that we have every meal to-gether and spend a week crammed together on a boat smaller than many New York City apart-ments, we do not ever talk about Edish. However, I'm sure that it is hard for Ken not to think of a boat trip to a summer destination in the snow as any-thing but a metaphor for this "wonderful" business I got him into.

April 19, 2009

Turning on my computer when I arrive home proves to be a mistake: There are several thousand emails. I have not missed my computer at all. Tony did all the cooking, so I am also home with an extra five pounds, which of course, helps my mood tremendously.

April 20, 2009

In response to my email asking him if we should try to stay open longer that our May 31 deadline, given the response to our sale, Don says, "You are finally home? Oh my god, no one has heard from you in nine days. We started to suspect foul play!"

I'm glad someone cares enough to worry. Don and I do our best to figure out how long it will take to sell as much china as we can. As we have been selling so much better than we expected, it is hard to know. Obviously, we don't want to be keeping our doors open and paying rent and salaries if we don't have money coming in. . .but we'd like to sell as much as we can.

Telling me that David has been in the back room, ranting to Francoise and everyone else that we have to sell much more, he says that they are all at the end of their rope. Working so hard, this is not what anyone wants to hear. After much back and forth, Don and I agree that mid-July seems like the best bet. Ken agrees. When I tell David that I would like to ask Wynonne if we can stay longer if that is acceptable to him, he more or less agrees but lets me know that Wynonne is a "disaster," and that it might be hard to talk to her.

I call and leave messages for Wynonne at work and on her cell.

As with any job, my first day back from vacation is hell; I spend it dealing with the stresses and tensions at both stores, which have only increased while I was gone. At some point during the day, I tell Don that I hate china. He responds, "Aw, I don't want to hear that. I love my china as much or more than ever. A job is one thing—a spoon lasts forever."

Kathi tells me that "things are getting weird around here." When I ask her to elaborate, she says, "This process is far from bringing out the best in people. . .understandable, I guess. It's giving me a perpetual headache, though. . . . So David hired Francoise to buy, huh? Interesting."

I knew, when the news about Francoise hit, that people would have feelings about it. But I can tell there's more, so I ask what she means about the rest.

She tells me that Sarah is crying, which is virtually impossible for me to imagine. Sarah is tough. She and Kathi have been working at a fevered pace to keep up with the way the sales floor looks. Most of our china was in rows of huge shelves in giant stacks. As things sold, Sarah and Kathi were moving things down from the top shelves (which were above shopper's heads except for the one time Hakeem Olajuwon came in—he didn't buy anything, but he did graciously give Kathi his autograph). They also filled in the gaps created by people buying things. It was the least glamorous job in the world—dusty, dirty, and hard. All of the sudden, Francoise had mobilized her team, and she and Aaron and Rose were out there moving things without consulting Sarah or Kathi.

These were not people sitting around, fighting over who got the next manicure. Every one of them was working hard and doing what they thought was best. They were fighting and crying over china display. Kathi said, "I am annoyed with just about everyone. . .I've learned a lot about my co-workers from this process." Me, too. Plus I learned something I'd always suspected—vacation is way better than real life.

Struggling about which battles to pick, I decide to ask Sarah if she is okay before I call Francoise. She replies, "Nope. But overruled and sleep deprived! I woke up about 1:30, obsessing over where we're going to move china, and couldn't get back to sleep until 5:30, so I'm loopy today." Kathi is right, in a way; this process is not bringing out the best in people. But it is interesting to notice some people working enormously hard and caring immensely about a job they know they are about to lose.

April 21, 2009

Still no response from Wynonne. Something strange is happening in our Salt Lake store. Mormonism is by far the dominant religion in Salt Lake City. They have something called Relief Society. My knowledge about this is mostly from what is transpiring in our store, so I may not have all the facts right.

As a reminder, the store is staffed by the big burly, bearded, tattoo-covered Jeremy (who was raised Mormon, also called "LDS," for Latter-Day Saints, but is no longer practicing); Lindsey, who was brought up in California and is learning about all of this along with me; and Craig, the Gender-Studies major.

From what I have seen, the Relief Society

seems to be made up of young women who have young children. Suddenly, every day, there were tons of them coming into the store in packs. Most of them were skinny, pretty, and blond, with several small children. The women were making cake stands from overturned glasses glued to dinner plates. They all get together to make their crafts one night, so they were shopping for supplies ahead of time.

Jeremy thought they were cute and funny, so he became the cake stand expert. First one of the women came and asked if we would give her a kickback if she brought all her friends in to do this. We said no. You cannot imagine how high-maintenance shoppers like this are. They want attention as they pull every plate and glass off the shelf. Next, they want to complain about the price. Then they buy one plate and one glass. This is not a Mormon issue; part of the reason that we know the drill is that, in both stores over the years, there have been projects like this one—usually inspired by Martha Stewart.

Typically, we fight over who has to help this kind of person. Not this time. Jeremy could spot them before they even made it into the store. They fell all over him. Hearing him pontificate about the merits of various plates and glasses, as the women listened intently, was hysterical. It broke up the day and gave us something to laugh about for a change. This went on for weeks.

Then one day, it just stopped.

April 22, 2009

Wynonne calls me back. Of course we can stay as long as we like, she tells me. Mid-July will be fine. She sounds scattered and worried. Telling me that the DA has called someone who wrote a letter in support of them, she says the letter writer was the former federal prosecutor. The DA asked him if he would like to come down and look at the evidence against them. He declined, thank you very much. Wynonne thinks that this is proof that the DA is gunning for them inappropriately. She says she really thinks they will get probation. Pleading guilty to a felony is her biggest regret, she tells me, because now she will be unable to vote. I tell her that I will see her in a week. Her sentencing is on the 28th. I will arrive the day before.

After I get off the phone with her, I tell Jeremy and Lindsey that we are going to stay open until mid-July. I assume that this will be welcome news, since no one has found a job. Lindsey goes off the deep end, screaming at me at the top of his lungs; we have a huge argument that leaves me literally shaking. He tells me how disorganized and awful I am, and that he needs to know an exact date that we will be finished; he needs closure.

Trying to understand what the issue is, I realize that this is mostly about the bonus I promised him and several other people if they stay until the end. When he tells me that I said I would give him the bonus if he stayed until May 31, I reply that I chose my words carefully at the time because I was shooting for May 31, but never having gone out of business before, I was not sure how this would work. Although we are swamped and he is under a huge amount of pressure, his outburst strikes me as extreme. Trying to keep in mind that he is worried about his future and floundering about where and what to do next, I remind myself that he has also been the one to be on time every day and stay past closing to pick up loose ends.

For the last several years we have arranged everyone's schedule around Craig's schooling. His plan is to move to London to be with Ian after he graduates in May. Between school and being goofy in love Craig, has not been focused on Edish. Much of the hard work in the past several months has fallen to Lindsey. Jeremy's life has a ton of drama, and I have not exactly been the queen of usefulness around the Salt Lake store. One thing that does not occur to me until later is that, of course, if he quits, he cannot file for unemployment. All of this is pent up in Lindsey's response.

Rationally I know this. But his anger is so visceral that it is terrifying.

Craig is at school, so it is just me, Lindsey, and Jeremy in the shop. Jeremy becomes the quietest I've ever seen him. It seems as if he is not even breathing. I agree to give Lindsey the bonus on May 31 and tell him he does not need to stick around after that; I will find someone else. We both know that would be awful for me, but I am willing to do it because I do not want to live through another confrontation like this. Lindsey goes out for a breath of fresh air (not a cigarette, because he is quitting, which I am sure has nothing to do with this outburst), and Jeremy tells me that he does not feel the same way at all and that he is happy to have the job; he promises that, no matter what, he will stick around until the bitter end. He knows that I need him, and he loves working for me.

Craig arrives from school. No one says a thing, and we barely talk to each other for the rest of the day. Lindsey does apologize in private.

Worried about how everyone else will take the news, I am very careful to tell each person in such a way that they know that they don't have to stay if they don't want to. Everyone in Houston treats me as if I'm nuts. They are all worried about finding a job and are thrilled to have the opportunity to work longer. Go figure.

April 24, 2009

Kerry emails me a story that Channel 2 ran in Houston today:

HOUSTON—*John Zielinski and Nancy Caho are among the hundreds of people who say they were victims of a Houston high-society scandal.*

It's alleged that the crime netted $3.5 million.

The accused are a husband and wife who, until recently, lived in a $1.5 million home in a West Houston neighborhood. It was a home complete with private lakes and tree-lined streets.

Investigators say that the couple worked at an auction house that catered to Houston's elite. And that they sold millions of dollars of fine china, furniture, and art.

They are the Harts of what had been Hart Galleries.

Jerry Hart appeared many times on TV, promoting upcoming sales and, in 1999, giving insight into art theft.

"Invariably there are thefts of art and art objects every day," said Hart during one TV appearance.

The auction house thrived for years. The Harts enjoyed a sterling reputation among the rich and not-so-rich, who all trusted the Harts to sell their valuables. But around 2003, something strange began happening, said Caho.

"Well, I didn't hear from them for many weeks," she said.

Caho said that the Harts auctioned an antique table for her for $3,000, but weeks later she still hadn't received the money.

She said that the Harts told her the table didn't sell.

Fehling: "That it didn't sell?"

Caho: "That it didn't sell. And I said, 'It did sell, because I was there and saw it sell.'"

Likewise, the Harts auctioned furniture and antiques for John Zielinski and his wife.

They were expecting to get $20,000.

"And I said, 'Where's our money?' And they said, 'We're having difficulty collecting some of the checks,'" said Zielinski.

The next thing Harts' customers learned was that the couple was bankrupt.

Cynthia Jones, who said she was a victim, confronted Jerry Hart.

"He was teary-eyed. We were teary-eyed. And I said, 'Jerry, you knew you were going to file for bankruptcy when you came out to my house.' And he said, 'Yes I did,'" said Jones.

Caho, Zielinski and Jones say that they felt betrayed, but assumed the Harts were just bad *business people.*

It wasn't until another victim, who expected $100,000 for a painting, tipped the Harris County DA that something wasn't right.

An investigation led to felony charges of theft and money laundering, and now the Harts have reached a plea deal on a charge of "misapplication of fiduciary property."

The Harts' attorneys would not comment other than to say the Harts were sloppy bookkeepers and didn't even use a computer.

The pair is supposed to be sentenced on Tuesday, but they do have supporters.

One Houston friend said he knows in his soul that the Harts didn't intend to cheat anyone. The victims have written letters, too.

Cynthia Jones' letter says: "I would rather had a burglar come into my house in the middle of the night."

John Zielinski's read: "We need to get our money back. If we don't, that's fine, but they need to go to jail."

Other stations run similar stories.

April 27, 2009

We are planning to send out an email saying that we are going to stay open until mid-June, and, per Wynonne's advice, that we are extending our 50%-off sale. On the plane to Houston, I work on the email, but of course I am preoccupied with tomorrow's sentencing hearing so the best I can come up with is:

> Subject: *I'll Be Seeing You.*
>
> As always, we cannot thank our customers enough for your continued support during our closing sale. Due to the overwhelming response to our going out of business sale, we have decided to extend our closing date to mid-July. We still have your pattern in stock at 50% off our originally low prices. All items are first-come, first-serve, and things are flying out of both of our stores, so don't wait! As our inventory decreases, we know that many of you are faced with buying our items that are not in like new condition. If you are concerned about purchasing the less than perfect items in your pattern, according to one customer, "If it has 'moderate wear,' I would still give it to the Queen instead of an iPod."
>
> We deeply appreciate the outpouring of good wishes so many of you have expressed. As a side note, many of the Edish elves are still looking for employment and would appreciate any leads.
>
> Thank you so much for all of your good wishes!

When I arrive at Edish, I am shocked at how good everything looks. We have sold almost half our stock, and if you had never been in the shop, the empty spaces would not be obvious. Many people have been working really hard to keep it looking good, and I know that is not because they have any extra time.

My friends Fred and Josie have a shop across the aisle from Edish, and I stop to catch up with them. Fred has known Wynonne for twice as long as I have. Since he is going to the hearing tomorrow, we decide to go together. The Harts, he tells me, have done nothing to plan for the possibility that they could go to jail tomorrow. Now they are rushing around, putting him and another dealer in the building on the checking account, and signing documents to give Fred and the Harts' son Trevor the power to make various business decisions for them if they do go to jail.

Although Wynonne is distraught and I can tell that it is suddenly hitting her that jail time is a possibility, she takes the time to introduce me to Trevor, a young man who lives in New York City and seems bright and poised. She and I talk for a few minutes; I tell her that I will take her out for a drink tomorrow night. Her eyes say something different, but she tells me that she is confident that things will work out in their favor.

The Edish folks look worn down with their own problems. And everyone has found out that David is hiring Francoise. People are cranky about it, but mostly what I hear is that they understand that Francoise cannot afford to be without a job.

Chapter Seven

*"The red color in Fiesta Ware was
achieved by adding uranium oxide in the
glaze—measurements have indicated that
by weight, up to 14% of the glaze might be
uranium. . . . Since this uranium could be
used in the production of an atomic bomb,
Fiesta red became a victim of World War
II when the US government confiscated
the company's stocks of uranium." [9]
—Berkeley Center for Cosmological
Physics website*

April 28, 2009

Fred picks me up. He is, as always, a font of information. On the way downtown he tells me that
he assumes this is a career-making case for the DA
because, instead of just letting the Harts know that

they were going to be arrested, she arrived at their house early in the morning with several camera crews from local TV stations. I flash back to their mug shots, which were splattered all over the news at the time. Although I did not know Wynonne well back then, I remember being shocked that she seemed to have no makeup and messy hair—not her style.

He goes on to say that the Harts have tried to settle with many of these people, but that they were unwilling to do so. Texas has a homestead law that allows people to keep their homes, no matter what, if they are in financial trouble. Nonetheless, the Harts sold their home to try to pay people back.

Once we get to the courtroom, Fred points out the various players. The room is full of supporters and detractors. And a lot of other people. And reporters.

Several hours pass as other people are being sentenced. Virtually all of them are for drug-related offenses, and almost everyone gets some jail time. It makes me wonder if this is the best use of our court and police resources. All of the people involved, except the attorneys, look miserable.

Trevor is there, and Fred points out the Harts' other two children—a son who is a college student, and a daughter who is married and lives outside the state. I wonder whether, if I was in the same position, I would want my kids there.

After various court maneuvers, the Hart case is called.

Fred and I have been sitting there hoping that Wynonne would not make a statement, because we are worried that she will say the wrong thing and harm herself. But both Wynonne and Jerry make statements. Jerry goes first. Apologizing for what he has done, he says, among other things, that he has a great money-making idea. If only he is granted probation, he believes he can be successful and make restitution. It is not perfect, but he does a pretty good job.

Then comes Wynonne's turn. Fred and I exchanged panicked looks. She starts by apologizing, taking full responsibility for everything that happened, then goes on to detail their charity work. Talking about how they had done virtually every charity auction they were asked to do, donating thousands of hours of their time, that they had been good to their employees (keeping them on the payroll when they became seriously ill, etc.), and listing various other good things that they had done, she asks for mercy. She is unfocused and rambling, but it could have been a lot worse.

Then their attorneys speak fairly eloquently about how they have never been in trouble before, about how they sold their house to try to make amends, about what fundamentally decent people they are, and about the hardships that prison would entail for individuals their age. Wynonne's attorney also talks about how much they have already lost, not just monetarily but in terms of their friends, their standing in the community, and having to go through this in front of their children.

Things seemed to be going pretty well. I try to read the judge's expression, to no avail.

Next it is the DA's turn. She rips everything they said to shreds. Calling what they have done a classic Ponzi scheme, she goes on to talk about a statement each of the Harts had written to the judge; she says that Jerry even admitted to robbing Peter to pay Paul. One of their former employees made a statement that she had been told by them to tell consigners that items had been sold for significantly less than was actually the case, she says. As an example, she speaks of someone who thought that their item sold for $5,000 and when it had really sold for $50,000. I can barely breathe.

She describes a man who had wanted to buy their business years before who had told her that it was being run unethically even then. Her point is clear: These are not nice people, and this was not an oversight or a one-time thing. She makes a big deal about the Harts living high on the hog and about the extravagant wedding they threw for their daughter several years ago. Their daughter visibly cringes.

I cannot see the Harts' faces at this point, and that is just fine with me.

When she is finally done, it is the judge's turn to talk. He looks at the DA and asks her when the last time was that they saw each other. It was a long time ago. They agree that they have not discussed this case in private. It seems an odd thing to be emphasizing. Then he says that he is asking because he can't believe how similar his remarks are going to be to the DA's.

I am no legal genius, but I am pretty sure that is not a good sign.

Continuing, he says that this is the most difficult case he has ever had. He declares that he has read every letter from their supporters and their detractors, and that he has also read the Harts' letters to him very carefully. Clearly he has not been moved by them. Pointing out that Jerry's letter was eight pages single spaced, he says that Jerry blamed everyone but himself. He is glad that they have both taken the blame in their speeches to him today, because that was not his impression from their letters; they helped themselves by taking responsibility today, he says.

Much of the rest really does sound like what the DA has said. This is a classic Ponzi scheme. It is

not credible that you didn't know that you were
supposed to have a separate accounts for consignors' items. This was a big part of the case and
what they pled guilty to. At some point while the
Harts were in business, the law changed, and they
were supposed to set up a separate checking account
for items that had sold at auction. Consignors
whose items had been sold were supposed to be paid
out of that account. Instead, the Harts put everything into one account and paid both the people
who had sold things at auction, and the light bill,
out of the same account—presumably not always
in that order.

Eternal optimist that I am, I still think they
might get a light sentence until he says, "You, sir,
are a thief in a suit, and you, ma'am, are a thief in
a dress."

They are sentenced to fourteen years in prison,
sentences to begin immediately.

They are led away, expressions of utter shock
on their faces. Their daughter leaves the courtroom
in tears. Fred suggests we depart quickly.

Back at the Antique Pavilion, everyone seems
to know that I had been at the hearing. The whole
building is abuzz. Trevor arrives, and I give him a
big hug though we just met yesterday. Whatever
his parents were expecting, fourteen years had
never occurred to them. They are thunderstruck,

he says. Apparently his parents' attorneys told him that the dehumanization process would start right away. They would take away all of their belongings and start treating them like prisoners. Trying to picture Wynonne going through all of this without a cigarette is nearly impossible. My emotions are swirling, I am shocked at the extent of their malfeasance, and yet I don't want them to go to prison.

Edish and its problems don't seem so huge at the moment—but I do return to them.

That night we go out to celebrate Chelby's birthday. Don, Leonard, Chelby, and I have fancy Mexican food and margaritas at Hugo's, a fabulous upscale restaurant. I vow not to discuss the hearing or anything Harts-related because it is not really birthday-party conversation, but they all want to know every detail. Although I know this sounds trite, all day long I have been feeling grateful for my freedom, for all the little things I take for granted: being able to go to the bathroom when I want to, brush my teeth, order a margarita (not right after brushing my teeth). Everything.

April 29, 2009

At the shop there is still a lot of chatter about the Harts. Trevor has stepped in and seems to be handling the chaos pretty well. Apparently, the

Harts really didn't think they were going to jail and so hadn't left him with much in the way of useful documents. Many other dealers in the Pavilion seem to be circling like vultures. I gather that a bunch of people don't have signed leases. They are mad and planning to use this to try to get reduced rent.

Since I need to be focusing on my own little issues, I am glad, for once, to mind my own business as it were. Our email is working. Sales are not overflowing as much as they did after the first 50%-off email, but I am amazed at how right Wynonne was. Things are flying out the door. Francoise and Aaron are helping Jamario ship; the rest of the gang is answering the phones or helping customers. Many shoppers continue to express their sympathy, and a few ask for a bigger discount. Back to hyper mode. Although we have gotten good at it, most of us are running on empty. Very few Edish elves have anything extra left to give.

Don and I decide to send a post card to our customers. Years ago, when our business was better, he and I used to spend hours coming up with ideas for holiday post cards. Especially in the years before email, they were very effective. We would hash out an idea and hire the best photographer we knew, David Farias, and the best graphics person on the planet, Donnette Reil, and send out an oversized post card. Some were better than others, of course. My favorite was China Beach. The three of us hauled a ton of china to Galveston, planted it halfway in the sand, and waited for the perfect sunset moment.

The most controversial was called "David Has the Perfect Gift." Plates and gravy boats were swirling around Michelangelo's David. There was a strategically placed bread-and-butter plate, although David joked that it should be a large platter. Usually we would get a great response from the card, as well as lots of phone calls about how clever it was. Not that time. The first three calls were quite negative and, though it was years ago, I remember word for word what the first caller said: "Take me off your mailing list! I don't want no neked man in my mail." At that moment, I was terrified that this would be the majority response. Fortunately, it was just the swiftest and most vocal. Most people thought it was hilarious.

Don and I knew that we did not have the budget or the time for our old-style postcard, so we had Donette work up a card with a yellow background (the Edish color) and bright print announcing that everything was 50% off. Just post card size, it was still going to be a fair amount of money to print and send, but Ken and David agreed it was worth doing because it would reach the people who hadn't heard via email, and reinforce it for those who had.

Mr. Waste-Forty-Minutes-Of-My-Time, times two, emails me to say that he is ready to talk about purchasing some things. He had asked for a list of our inventory, which was a bit of a chore, but Ken had done it anyway because I stupidly said it might be worth it, that the man might buy a fair amount. Fool me once, shame on you; fool me twice, shame on me; fool me three times, and it pretty much makes me a raging idiot. Moron. When I email him back, I foist him off on Kerry. Very classy of me.

Since he'd had the list for a month and we had been selling our inventory like crazy, the list was no longer accurate. Nonetheless, Kerry goes through and puts everything we still have that he wants into a sale. This takes hours. Kerry then gives him the total. He offers half of that—half of the half off we were already selling things for! Finally, having dealt with this man for months, I understand that this is a "life is too short" customer. Perhaps yet another indicator of my egregious lack of intelligence is that this took so long. "Just tell him, 'No thank you,'" I tell Kerry. The customer, of course, asks for another list. Kerry suggests telling him that we have worked up a list of our inventory just for him, and that it is called www.Edish.com.

I can only assume that Kerry was not rude enough, because this was not the last time we would hear from this fellow.

All of us are doing our own form of triage. Most worrisome to Kathi is that scores of people are complaining that they want to be removed from our emailing list. She has been doggedly pursing this tedious task, but it is hard to keep up. Hating that anyone is unhappy with us for any reason, she cannot stand to have it not be perfect—not to mention she wants to make sure we don't get black-listed.

I remind her that, when the phones are ringing off the hook, she needs to help customers more than clean up the mailing list, and that, at most, people will have to put up with two or three more emails from us. Spammers are repulsive, we can all agree on that (except the spammer's grandmother), but we are only emailing people who asked to hear from us at one time, and she has done a good job of deleting them as people ask her to. If a few people have to hit delete three more times, is that the end of the world? We've had this argument over and over again in the past seventeen years or so—never over the same topic, but always taking the same sides. She wants to do a perfect job; I want her to do a mediocre one, so it will go faster. I muse that this might be the last time.

My friend Mathilde and I go out for martinis and the Harts' sentencing hearing recap one more time. Yet again, I wonder what Wynonne is having for dinner. Mathilde remains my friend despite the fact that I gave her terrible advice years ago, which she took. "Ask for it," I told her. "No one ever got fired for asking for a raise." So she did. And she *did* get fired. Although we are still close, you will not hear her asking for my opinion about anything important.

April 30, 2009

I am going home today, which works out nicely because I start my day with my husband calling to inform me that he found out, when he went to drop the kids off at school on his way to work, that the Park City schools are closed for a week due to confirmed cases of swine flu, 'cause that's just what we all need.

I wonder if my next job will understand when I call up and say, "Can't come to work for a week because the schools are closed."

My in-laws volunteer to take the kids for the day while I am traveling home. Neither one of them is in great health, so I always worry about exposing them to my germy kids, but they are from the Greatest Generation (my father-in-law was wounded at Iwo Jima), so they don't believe in the swine flu. They never catch anything.

When I go to the shop for a little while before I catch my plane, David asks me about our reference books. Our collection of books about china is outrageous. Over the years we have saved boxes and boxes of old catalogs from china companies to use as reference materials and bought every book about china known to mankind. He would like to buy some of them; I feel like asking why, since he has told me that he is not going into the china business, but instead tell him that he can buy whatever he wants.

Don emails me:

> It is hard to watch this. Not five minutes after you left, David came down here to ravage the library, and he is still doing it. He has a cart for books he wants and books that Edish can sell, I guess. He has our huge trash can, and he is throwing away what he thinks is trash, and then he is piling other stuff in the giveaway box. For what it is worth, I don't think he should be doing this. You told him to take what he wanted. That is all he should be doing. I know it's minor, but it stinks.

And then, half an hour later:

> Don't worry about my previous email. I'm sure I overreacted. Plus I got the things I wanted out of the trash and the giveaway.

Don and I have had a sordid history of dumpster diving. Our best haul was four giant bags full of what we can only assume are Frank Lloyd Wright-designed lighting fixtures out of the dumpster next to the Guggenheim Museum in New York. We carried them around Manhattan all day. They were heavy. (Don, if you're reading this, where are those? They are half mine!)

He goes on to say:

> He kept some of the better, newer, more comprehensive or valuable ones, but I own nearly every one of those I would want, and I got to buy the things I wanted. I'm just so glad I was here today to save some of these things for my library and archives.

Are we old enough to have libraries and archives? All I have is an overcrowded book shelf from Ikea. . .but I'm glad all's well that ends well.

On the plane, as I decompress, I think about all the arcane knowledge we all have stored in our heads. Yes, bone china really does have cow bones in it. No, you should not listen to your mother-in-law when she tells you to pick out the simple china pattern so you won't get tired of it. In fact, this might be the second-worst piece of advice that is consistently given to brides. You should pick out something you love, because the chances are you will still love it twenty years later. This is china-picking advice, but it may work for picking the groom, too.

Also, if you buy collector plates as an investment, you might just as well pack up your money and send it to Bernie Madoff. And modern martini glasses are huge compared to the ones from the thirties. And the original saucer champagne glasses probably really were modeled on a woman's breast, and make great martini glasses.

I know that Raymond Loewy designed patterns for Rosenthal china as well as a Studebaker and the original Coke bottle, and that Russell Wright was the Martha Stewart of his day—he and his wife Mary designed dishes, furniture, lamps, and more—and that people, tired of all those florals and antiques, ate up their modern designs. Any china that says *Warranted 22-Karat Gold* on it is old but was cheap and poorly made when it was new and is still cheap and poorly made (sorry if you have been planning on that set of china to pay for your retirement).

Stolen china is almost always taken by relatives. I learned this over years of being in the china business, and I have no idea what it says about our society. First of all, people who have had something stolen, whether it was ten years ago or yesterday, always assume that the china on our shelves is theirs. Lenox China has made the Autumn pattern since 1919 and has made gazillions of pieces, but people who have had it stolen from their homes are sure that the pieces on our shelf belong to them. And they are irate when I won't just turn it over.

Our records are excellent, so we always know whom we bought things from and are happy to tell anyone who asks. The last thing we want is to buy stolen merchandise or develop a reputation as people who will. Invariably, someone will tell us that we bought it from their daughter or son, and that it belonged to them. Our policy has been that, if the person files a police report, we will give it to the police and take the loss. But people rarely want to turn in their kids and often seem furious that we won't just return their china. Over the last twenty years, I have had this conversation about eight times. We let people buy it at our cost and work it out themselves with their kids if that is what they want.

I have learned as well that, yes, you should mix and match your china if you like that look, that Royal Albert Old Country Roses is the most popular china pattern in the world, and that they have made almost everything you can imagine in it, including a telephone. We have sold three of them over the years, though I would not be caught dead with one.

It is true that I suggested to Martha Stewart that an old porcelain chamber pot could be used as a popcorn bowl. She did not use the word "gross" because she has too much class but was nonetheless able to convey that word with one look.

I have learned that the Ricardos' pattern on *I Love Lucy* was Franciscan Ivy, that Woodrow Wilson was the first president to use American china (Lenox, of course), that the so-called Nazi china platter in the movie *American Beauty* sure looked to me like a piece of Lenox (which was made in Trenton, New Jersey, not in Germany) with a swastika painted on it.

I think of the scores of people who asked if we had their "out of print" china pattern. The look: There is a certain look a man has when he comes into the shop, usually in a business suit, and asks if we have what he is looking for. They think they are unique, but they aren't; they are finally ready to buy that piece of their mother's they broke when they were kids and playing baseball, football, or anything else with a ball in the house. You know, the one with the pink flowers. This is an inside china joke: Whenever we had a new employee, I would call them and ask if they have my pattern— "you know, the one with the pink flowers." The rest of us thought this was hilarious. None of us has counted, but there must be 10,000 patterns with pink flowers, and every few months we would get a customer who was quite irritated with us because we didn't know what they meant when they were looking for the one with the pink flowers.

Chapter Eight

*"She [Emily Post—they were having
an argument via letter in* Time *magazine
in 1946] stands for drinking tea gracefully
from a fine flaring cup (I suppose with the
pinky raised—with nary a drip). Tell
Emily I stand for more drooling, less fancy
'etiquette' and less housework."*[10]
—Russell Wright

May 1, 2009

Thanks to the swine flu epidemic, I need to stay
home with my children, which is why I need to put
out the next fire via email. Our latest email blast
has been yet again quite effective. Consequently,
all hell is breaking loose in Salt Lake City. Jeremy,
our shipper, seems to have his hands full with his
life. He has not come to work or called for two

days. Legally, my understanding is that one more day of this is considered job abandonment. Personally, I think it is also just plain obnoxious, and, this close to the end, I would rather not have to train a new shipper.

Craig emails me to ask if I will email Jeremy and let him know that we are expecting him to work a full day Monday. That doesn't seem like too much for Craig to ask from me, or, frankly, for me to ask of Jeremy. When I email him, he responds with his usual:

> *Just being amazing! You? I have had to turn my phone off, so I wasn't able to email or text anyone. I am here, it is good. Also, splitting my last advance over the next two paychecks would be cool, thanks again.*

Although I understand that the generation behind me is considerably more casual than I am about many things, I assume one is still supposed to either show up for work or call. And perhaps this is out of line, but it occurs to me that, having failed to do this for two days, asking to spread out your previous advance longer than agreed upon might not be appropriate. But what do I know?

I respond by reminding him that he has not

come to work or called in two days. I am not making this up—this is his response:

> *I don't have a way to directly communicate with you. If you could leave me a number, that would be great. I need it anyways to put it on some applications for a work reference.*

I should've replied, "Don't let the door hit you on the way out." What I said—knowing that I was going to be home for days with my kids, that we were short-handed and busy, and that, despite his behavior, he really needed the money—was:

> *But you do have a way to call work; did you? Did anyone know you weren't coming in? I know it seems really loose at Edish, and in some ways it is, but we do need to know if you are not able to come to work.*

Seems kind of basic to me. His response?

> *My bad. I do get the fact that I should have made more of an effort to let Edish know.*

Special.

May 7, 2009

Park City schools re-open, and I am able to return to work. Jeremy has gotten us caught up on shipping, which is a good thing for several reasons.

May 8, 2009

Jeremy gets his small paycheck (due to his low hours and previous advance) and asks for another advance. In a show of extreme intelligence, I give it to him.

People are still responding to our latest email.

Don lets me know that the post cards are ready to be picked up from Donette; he wants to know if he can go ahead and write a check for the full amount. This is the first time we have ever been able to pay in full for her services. Going out of business sure is cool.

May 11, 2009

Craig tells me that he is not going to stay until the end. After he finishes school at the end of May, he will stay an extra two weeks, but that is it. He is in love and eager to move to London to be with the love of his life and start working towards citizenship.

Although I understand his sense of urgency, I am also irritated. For the last several years, I have worked around and hired around his schedule, so that he could finish school. The least he could do is give me an extra month.

However, this hasn't been fun to say the least, and he and Lindsey are at each other's throats, so I appreciate his position. And I wonder if things might be better with Lindsey and Jeremy when they don't feel Craig's irritation and condescension at every move.

Weighing a new, exciting life in London against another month at grubby Edish can't have been that hard a decision—although, since he and Ian have only ever spent a week at a time together, I can't help but wonder if this whole thing might backfire.

May 14, 2009

The post card that we spent about $25,000 on has gone out, and the response is tepid at best. I wish that we had not spent the money.

May 15, 2009

Or that I had a little patience. We are back on the roller-coaster of crazy giant sales, which, as usual, brings its own set of problems.

May 18, 2009

Our Salt Lake City store has a basement that we use to store china, mostly duplicates of what we have upstairs. A large chain across the stairs lets customers know that they are not to go down there. It is dark and dank. Lindsay has been bringing lots of china up, as he has extra time. Hard work, it is along the lines of Kathi in the Houston store carrying china from our upstairs back room.

Lindsey tells me that Craig has told him that he should not be spending his time this way. I'm not sure why, since it needs to be done. Tensions are flying high at the shop, so if one of them says white, the other says black. I make a point of telling Lindsey, in front of Craig, that I appreciate him doing this, and that the rest needs to be brought up when they have time. I can tell as soon as I say it that Lindsey thinks I am giving him direction. And he does not like to be told what to do. I know that I have set him off, and that I will pay.

May 19, 2009

Lindsey sends me an email on which he cc's some attorney I have never heard of. All of us are under a lot of stress, but this strikes me as pretty over the top given that we already had this conversation a couple of weeks ago when I made it clear that we were staying open until mid-July. The email reads:

> *Do you know when our last day is yet? Up*
> *until last Friday, according to your website and*

many emails sent to me from Edish, what you told
me back in February, we would be open until "the
end of May." Now it says the middle of July. Is
it the middle of July, Miriam? Please select a date
and stick with it, and let's move forward to hit
that date rather than what we have been doing.
You do know there are laws that protect employ-
ees regarding closures and "due notice," which is
sixty days. Pretty soon, it's not gonna be the mid-
dle of May anymore, and I'm done asking you
about this. You've had plenty of time to do it.
The next step for me, if you cannot or will not do
this, is to go to the other owners you are suppos-
edly in business with.

I wish he would. Why should I have all the fun?
He goes on to say:

I don't think anyone needs to be patronized,
do they? All the bullshit back stock being taken
up and shelved, having the shelves themselves re-
organized—I know when it needs to come up, and
I know when to do it. I don't need you to come
over and tell me that.

I assume this is the real issue. He does not want
even the hint of anyone, including the person he
works for, telling him what to do.

When I send his email to Don, because I am wondering if I am missing something, he replies:

> *Why has Lindsey taken this sudden turn for the mean? He is a free agent and can leave work anytime he wants. If he tentatively agreed to stay until May 31 because he wants a bonus, he does that. If he doesn't want to do that now, then he doesn't have to. What is the problem? Nobody signed a contract. In fact you left it open ended, which is actually better for the employees, I think. You said you wanted employees to stay, but that you would understand if they left because an opportunity came up.*

Feeling a little less insane, I tell Don that I am feeling like firing Lindsey but it would be really hard because we are so busy. He responds:

> *I agree. I would get rid of him. I would tell him that all of his hard work is appreciated. That yes, the store is going to have to stay open longer, it is not a secret or a plot to indenture employees. You have never had to go out of business before, and some of the decisions have to be made during the closing process. He was still eligible to receive his bonus for staying until the end of May as you had agreed to, but now he is fired and not eligible.*

Hand him a check for his hours worked and his
earned vacation.

Don is right. Nonetheless, I email Lindsey and
tell him that we have already had this conversation,
that he knows that we are closing later than
planned, that I have already agreed to give him his
bonus at the end of May, which I have not agreed
to do for anyone else, and that if he is done with
Edish, perhaps it is time for him to go now, or at
the end of May, because even though I dread having to train someone new so close to the end, I am
feeling very much at the end of my rope. And I tell
him that he is the only employee who has objected
to us staying open longer.

Lindsey responds by telling me that he doesn't
want to leave, and, regarding bringing things up
from the basement: "The truth is, I've been doing
what I see fit for a while here, and the store looks
good, is in shape, is clean, because it was driving
me crazy that nobody else seemed to care. I did."

He does have a point. And he thinks I am not
aware that he spends a lot of time at work, some
times hours a day, surfing the Internet.

We both agree to communicate better and then
he says: "Thanks, Miriam. Sorry for riding your
tail so hard. I'm really tired of being so stressed out
by these things. Losing your job and relocating is

very stressful."

True. Obviously, he has been talking to Jeremy, because the next email I get is from him. You may remember that he was there for the blowup that Lindsey and I had on this topic a few weeks ago. At the time he said that he understood that I had said that the bonus was to be given when we closed, not a specific date, and that it didn't matter to him because he was planning on staying until the end. Things change.

> *Miriam, it's Jeremy. Hey, I have a couple of questions about the stay-to-the-end bonus. I was told by you that it would be paid on May 31. I understand that you and the other owners have decided to prolong that date to the middle of July. So are you not going to give me the bonus I was promised on May 31? If not, why? Also, if is until July, does that mean that I am getting more of a bonus? Please let me know about this as soon as possible. Thanks, Jeremy.*

Well, at least there was no attorney cc'd on this one.

We go back and forth a few rounds on this, with him saying he did not remember discussing this, and me agreeing to give him the bonus on May 31, and, predictably, him asking for another bonus

to stay till the bitter end. After I refuse, he promises to stay until we close anyway.

Lest it seem that Salt Lake is the only place
falling apart at the seams, Sarah sends me an email
from Houston telling me that she was just back
from a great day off but:

> *Apparently WW III has broken out here.*
> *Management is on a tear against Don, and I've*
> *been told to tell you that Francoise in not going to*
> *help Don clean out his office because he won't start*
> *doing anything now (no one had asked her to clean*
> *out his office). They [Francoise and Kerry, I as-*
> *sume] are both really unhappy with him and irri-*
> *tated. I'm not letting them ruin my good mood,*
> *though.*

Me neither.

May 23, 2009

The postcard is working its magic. We have a
huge day, and everyone is worn out.

Craig's last day is in a couple of weeks, and I am
starting to get the inkling that Jeremy is not going
to stay much past the moment he gets his bonus, in
spite of his repeated assurances to the contrary. I
panic. My stepson has a close friend, a roller-blad-
ing superstar who has traveled all over the world to

compete. Much to his parents' relief, he has moved back to Utah to finally resume his education. He is job hunting; I have always adored him, so I am reluctant to hire him. If he spends a month and half with me in this state, I will never see him again. Desperation wins out, though, and I ask Cameron if he would like to work for us until the end.

May 28, 2009

Cameron agrees to take the job. He will start June 2. I have no idea how lucky I am.

Trevor sends me an email to let me know that his parents have hired new lawyers and today they are having a hearing for a motion for a new trial; they will have more information within the next forty-five days. I can't imagine what could happen to change the outcome. Hopefully, they are not throwing good money after bad. Since he hasn't asked for an opinion from my brilliant legal mind, but he has asked me to keep my fingers crossed, I tell him I will. He also lets me know how great Don is. Guess he didn't get the memo from Kerry and Francoise.

May 30, 2009

People have been ordering like crazy on the web and putting sweet messages in the comments sections about how much they will miss us. Today someone says:

> *I thought I'd ordered my last, but at these*
> *prices, I'm going to eat off my Wedgwood during*
> *the week. Good luck in the future.*

Don tells me about a lady who told him the reason we don't have any more of her Franciscan pattern is that it is very rare, since the factory was bombed in the war. Since Franciscan was made in California, he goes on to say that not a lot of people remember those air raids over Los Angeles in the 1940s. I know he is trying to cheer me up, and I appreciate it.

This engenders a conversation about things various people have told us over the years: the man who told us that his china was so old it had "Civil War dirt" on it, the lady who told us that her father brought back Noritake that he had stolen out of a cave in Japan in World War II (it was a pattern that was sold in the PX after the war), the eighty-seven-year-old lady who came in to sell us her Castleton Sunnyvale (the most popular discontinued pattern of all time, a colorful floral china). It was not at all unusual for someone that age to sell us things as they downsized, but she was putting the money towards a "new" set—a different Castleton pattern, discontinued, naturally, since Castleton went out of business in the 1970s. We gently inquired if we could ask why she was doing this.

Gloria, a gray-and-white pattern, was the one that she had wanted when she got married, but her mother had insisted that she get the more popular Sunnyvale. She went on to say, "My mother is dead now, and I can do whatever I want."

We are reminded of the dealer in her nineties who was selling RS Prussia (expensive hand-painted antique vases) on the Internet in 1999 when we were struggling to get our website going. She asked me if I understood how the Internet worked. Not being Al Gore, I told her that I did not. Her reply: "Well, I do. It's magic."

We recall the difficult, elderly customer who decided she liked us after we admired her vintage red-white-and-blue Peter Max eyeglasses. A docent at Bayou Bend, one of the best American Decorative Arts museums in the world, she took Don and me on personal tour and out to lunch. It was fabulous. And to this day (and in spite of our thank-you notes), she refers to us as Marian and Dan.

There will be some things I will miss about this.

June 1, 2009

And some I won't. Jeremy sends me an email to let me know that he is moving to California and, despite the fact that he does not yet have a job there, it is an emergency that he leave in ten days. Am I surprised that he is telling me this the day after he got his bonus to stay until the end? Well, frankly, I thought it might be a week; I am lucky Cameron starts tomorrow.

June 2, 2009

Cameron arrives just in time to save the day. We are swamped; he picks up shipping rapidly. We have a problem with a shipment that we have sent via UPS. When I look over and see he is on his cell phone, I think, *How twenty-something to talk on your cell phone on the first day of your new job.* It turns out he is on the phone to his sister, who works for UPS, resolving the problem.

Jeremy is clearly having personal problems and is distracted. My guess is that he is not going to even last the ten days he just told me he would. However, Cameron's youthful energy seems to shift what is happening in the store. He has figured out a way to get along with Craig and Lindsey and not take sides. And he is smart and picks things up quickly.

June 3, 2009

Don writes:

> *I have been remiss in telling you about something! Kathi has been an amazing force moving*

china in the shop. Every day she moves merch down from top shelves and up from bottom shelves. She unearths and features good-selling patterns, patterns that mix well with others, and patterns we still have good serving pieces in or still have plenty of dinners in, etc. It has made a real difference in sales. In addition to our straight pattern-matching business, much of our traffic for weeks has been people (impulse buyers) cruising through to see what they like and can use. Over and over I have seen things that I knew about on a shelf, that I was sort of keeping an eye on, get put into a better spot by Kathi, where it sells after that!

All the while during the moving, she cleans the merchandise up a little, dusts the shelves, and puts in the new location codes. She actually deserves a big pat on the back from all of us, but it would be especially nice I think to get some acknowledgment from you. It is a terrible, crawling on-your-hands-and-knees, breathing-dust-thanklessly job that she took on herself that she has been pecking away at for weeks now.

Naturally, I email Kathi to thank her for doing such a fabulous job and take all credit for the thinking to take time to thank her. I should run a huge company where all you do all day is take credit for other people's ideas and work.

Sales are starting to slow. Time to send a new letter with the next discount.

June 5, 2009

> Subject: Every Time We Say Goodbye.
> Dear So and So,
>
> Every time we say goodbye, I die a little,
> Every time we say goodbye, I wonder why a little . . . .
>
> All of you who have told us that you are anxiously awaiting the next markdown. . . here it is! Everything at Edish is 75% off!
>
> There is still a surprisingly good selection of patterns left! Come in now or shop the web and get things for twenty-five cents on the dollar!
>
> We will be completely gone soon! If you have been holding out for another major reduction on your pattern(s), this is it! We expect to have a huge response to this huge reduction!
>
> Thank you so much for all of your kind words during the last several months. You have no idea what they have meant to us.

June 6, 2009

The response is wild. And, of course it is a huge amount of work to sell china in these quantities. Our sales are nearly $10,000 today, which is a truck-

load at 75% off. Virtually every web sale is, as usual
these days, accompanied by very kind remarks. My
favorite of the day:

> *Thanks for all your help, and best wishes to*
> *all of you on your future endeavors. Glad to have*
> *the last of the Rochelle. It will look so classy at*
> *my funeral to have all those matching cups and*
> *saucers.*

June 8, 2009

Jeremy informs me that this is his last day.
And I get an email from Don:

> *Subject: Cheap People Are Cheap!*
> *A dealer that we have done business with for*
> *years called me to ask if he could have free ship-*
> *ping if he placed a substantial order at 75% off.*
> *Our shipping charge is ten dollars. And some*
> *lady asked him what her total was "up to now"*
> *before she would add to her order. She was up to*
> *$7.50.*

We are totally swamped, and there is just no
way that Cameron, who is practically a superhero,
and Lindsey, who is one, at the moment anyway,
can do all of this. Cameron has a girlfriend who is
visiting for the summer from Pennsylvania and has

been eating lunch with us. Since she seems as if she can walk and chew bubblegum at the same time, I ask her if she'd like to help us until the end; she can start tomorrow.

June 9, 2009

Kendall turns out be hardworking and responsible, becoming employee of the month on her first day. Lindsey says it is because she is young and enthusiastic and hasn't yet learned that there is no percentage in that.

When I tell Kerry that I am writing a book about this, he responds, "Have you considered writing a true crime book, starting with all of the felonious dealers David has championed or employed and ending with the downfall of our current landlords?" When I ask who, he reminds me of X, the person whose charges are still pending; and a close friend of David's, who was convicted of trafficking in stolen gravestones and other objects in New Orleans; and a few others. This isn't Kerry's typical rant. He goes on to say, "I'm just mad at David these days, what with him not wanting to take public credit for why we're going out of business (and holding himself up as such an 'honest' man while being so disingenuous). I just recalled the disapproving remarks David made to me years ago when I was talking on the sales floor and mentioned that my dad was thrilled because he had won the office football pool and it was in the hundreds of dollars. 'That's gambling, and that's illegal.' He hadn't rehired the felon at that point, and I can't remember if the grave robber had been caught yet or was in or out of prison."

June 10, 2009

Sarah emails me to say that they are so swamped she doesn't have time to go to the bathroom. I try not to think about the implications of that. Everything is really fine; they are in good shape, she tells me, "Although I have noticed that our customers our getting dumber as the price falls." We all have.

Amid the hundreds of emails and comments from web sales that we have gotten since the post card hit, we did get one person who said, "We are sad to hear that you are closing. But still are there other savings available on our pattern that we are not asking for?" You mean besides 75% off?

June 12, 2009

In the comments section of her websale, a customer writes, *I saw you on the Oprah Winfrey Show,* which is awesome since I was never on that show. If I had been, I doubt we would be going out of business.

And someone from Israel places an order and tells us that she has found out about us by "skiing on the Internet."

Don says, "It's a theme. The bottom feeder 75%-off people can't bear to pay the shipping cost of $5.00 or $10.00, and sometimes they just won't order! I had two today. What a strange reality they must have." The worst thing about him saying this is that I can absolutely imagine myself doing the same thing. Yuck.

He goes on to say, "The whole closing experience would make a great chapter in your book, but an even better psychological research paper."

Or, I think, a reality TV show.

Today is Craig's last day. We are swamped with the sale, but we have a little good-bye lunch. He was just barely twenty when he started ten years ago; we have been through a lot together over the years. Memories of me covering for him, so he could go to school and on a long vacation to Australia, float through my mind. So do ones of him stepping up to the plate for me when my twins were born (somewhere there is a photo of me nursing both kids while on the phone with Craig), when my husband had emergency open-heart surgery when my kids were two, and even before all that, handling everything when I got married in New

York and went on my honeymoon. He has really been there for the good, the bad, and the ugly. Don't even ask how much weight I gained when I was pregnant. Can I still call it pregnancy weight now that my kids are six?

Through the years, we have been through scads of employees. He worked with J., my first Salt Lake City employee, who had long dyed-black hair and the longest fingernails I've ever seen, and who loved to listen to The Cure all day (not exactly music to inspire china shoppers). J. now has a Ph.D. in Chemistry. Working with the Christian Fundamentalist who taught us about rapture, and whom we caught looking at porn on our computer, was a joy. As was working with all the people who thought I didn't know they were getting high in the parking lot when they went outside for a "cigarette."

Craig was there for the opening night party for Chinatown. Ken and Bruce had gone skiing at Snowbird that day, and when they called to say they were not going to make it to the party because an avalanche had blocked the road, I thought they were joking. They were not. It was Craig who explained to me that it was okay to have wine at that party, but that I'd better also have plenty of soft drinks on hand since Mormons don't drink. His advice about refraining from asking customers if they would like a cup of coffee was spot-on; I thought I was being polite, but Mormons don't drink coffee either.

Although we have had our struggles, I will miss him. I am glad that he is going to London to live happily ever after. He has started "taking afternoon tea" and talking about "the tube," and I predict that, within six months, he will have an English accent. I really hope he makes it to the six-month mark.

June 15, 2009

It is scary. We can't even keep enough foam peanuts to ship because we are using them so fast. There are piles of orders everywhere. This is a stellar time to have two brand-new shippers in Salt Lake. We forward the phones, but Rebecca tells me it is terrifying there, too. When I say that if anyone wants to know if there order has shipped, just tell them we don't know, and if they don't like it they can cancel their order, the only thing she can say is, "Yikes."

June 17, 2009

Everyone is working so hard just to keep our heads above water. In Salt Lake, Kendall and Cameron are busting out shipments and have changed the atmosphere of the store. Their youthful energy is contagious. Lindsey is being a really good sport about having to show them how to do everything. It does help that they pick things up very quickly.

We are all so overwhelmed that the last thing we need is another problem. So we get one. There is some kind of glitch in our email program. Kathi has been diligently removing people who have asked to no longer receive emails from us. Somehow, some of those she has taken off are still getting emails.

When I get an email that I don't want, I either delete it or click "report spam" in my email program. Three people find this too prosaic. Each day we are still getting twenty or more very sweet emails from people who were sorry that this was their last order and sad to see us go. But they didn't make up for the emails that Kathi received excoriating her for sending spam. As she said, "I don't think you pay me enough for this."

One man sent four separate emails—one calling us a spamming cocksucker and telling us to piss off, one telling us that he had Direct TV (not sure why that mattered) and to drop dead, one telling us to eat shit, and one with a violent pornographic image. I dislike spam as much as the next guy, but that seemed a bit much. The person who wrote STOP HARASSING ME!!!!!!!!!!!! seemed relatively mild after that. I did feel sorry for the person who wrote, *Well, you know what, she died for real May 1, 2009, so screw you and take us off your list. Fucking pig.* That person's email address included the handle *I'm a Catch.* I'm sure you are.

June 18, 2009

Just because everything is perfect, ADP doesn't send our payroll. This presents huge problems, and so, logically, I explode at Don. It is their mistake, not his, but he is the one who tells me, not them. I am mean and cranky. After he gets them to cancel the live checks (we have four people who don't want to have checks direct-deposited) and to resend the info for the direct-deposit ones, he accepts my apology for being a bitch. At some point early in the process of going out of business, I remember thinking that I was going to need to proceed in such a way that at the end, I could, at least, feel good about my behavior. Oh, well.

Then I get an email from a woman who writes:

> *I have enjoyed and appreciated your emails during this time of closure of your company. I am connected to you through my nephew Craig. We have enjoyed visiting him in the store and he has found some special dishes for us. We have especially appreciated the support you gave him while*

he was finishing work on his college degree. He just graduated a couple of weeks ago. We are sorry you are closing and wish you well with whatever comes next.

and one from someone who writes: *Using a little Cole Porter tune to sell your remaining stock. He would be so proud.*

I really doubt that, but it does cheer me up. As does the person who writes:

> *Why the gods above me, who must be in the know, think so little of me, they allow you to go. But if you must go, I will look tomorrow and spend every last cent I can. There's no love song finer, but how strange the change from major to minor. . .every time you say good bye.*

Kathi, whose timing is impeccable, sends me an email attachment with all of the kind emails people have sent. It is ninety-four pages long. I cry when I read through it.

Chapter Nine

*"All things look good from far away
and it is man's eternally persistent child-
like faith in the reality of that illusion that
has made him the triumphant restless
being he is."[11]*
—Rockwell Kent, Voyaging:
Southward from
the Straights of Magellan

June 19, 2009

My son Max wakes up with a terrible sore
throat and a 104°-plus fever. We are slammed at
work, but I don't have a choice, I have to stay home
and take him to the doctor. After I make the ap-
pointment, the doctor's office calls back to verify
the symptoms. They tell me to call from my car
when I get there and not to come in. A nurse meets

us outside with special masks for us to wear. She is dressed from head to toe in what looks like a hazmat suit. My poor son is so sick he can barely walk. They take us into a special room, where we wait for two hours. Feeling pretty punky myself, I am thrilled when the doctor looks at us and says, "I'm sure you both have swine flu." I ask her to do a strep test anyway, because Max's throat is so sore. The rapid test comes back negative.

After giving us a prescription for Tamiflu for each member of the family, she tells us to have no contact with anyone for seven days. Seven days. Spreading joy throughout the land, I can't wait to tell the Edish gang. Although I am worried about how they will make it, I am more worried about my son. He can barely lift his head. When I ask the doctor if I should go get my daughter from camp to keep from infecting the other kids, she says no. Of course, my daughter Madeleine comes down with the same thing the next day.

I arrive home to an email from Kathi telling me how stressed out and crabby everyone is, especially Sarah. She writes, *It's amazing how many people around here think that they are carrying the brunt of the process*, and that Sarah's behavior doesn't make Kathi want to give her any assistance. Five minutes later, she emails again: *Okay, so now I feel like a bitch. She apologized. Guess I'll help her some more.*

Truthfully, lots of people feel like they are carrying the brunt of this, because they are. There is so much to do, and it is so hard. When we opened, it was equally hard, but we were buoyed by a sense of hope for the future. Now we are trying to muster the same level of energy to quash everything we have worked so hard for. It reminds me of something my father says about my grandmother, who is becoming increasingly difficult to care for—she is as much work as a small child, but it is not rewarding the way it is with children, whom you can see growing and changing before your eyes. When we were opening and filled with hope, it was one thing to work this hard. But doing it now just sucks.

June 20, 2009

Someone places a web order for $2,491.97; I can only imagine what that looks like at 75% off.

As I am tucking my sick kids into bed, they ask me about their grandpa, who is in ill health but good spirits. Telling them that he has been close to death several times, I say that he feels lucky each day that he wakes up, and that he does his best to enjoy each day to its fullest. My son says, "Yesterday is history, tomorrow is a mystery, today is a gift. That is why it is called the present." Thinking that he may be the next Dalai Lama, my chest puffs out with pride when I ask, "Where did you hear that?"

Both kids look at me as if I am a moron as they say in unison, "Duh, *Kung Fu Panda*, Mom."

June 22, 2009

At 7 a.m., I get a frantic email from Lindsey, who is writing from work about how behind they are. Customers and staff from the Houston store calling to see if their orders have shipped yet, when we are just trying to keep up, creates its own whole weird set of problems. Naturally, I understand why people would be worrying about ordering from someone going out of business. Sarah is on the front lines hearing from these customers, so she is sending emails to Lindsey like *Get this shipped today.* Lindsey, who doesn't like to be told what to do on a good day, is furious. When I call Kerry to ask if I can have him handle all customer paperwork and refund issues for Salt Lake, since I can't do it from home because I don't have a credit card machine, he is happy to do it, and it seems to solve the problem.

More importantly to me, both of my kids are starting to act as if they are going to live. I've never been so happy to hear them complain about being bored. Two days ago, they could barely move. Every working mother has moments where guilt and responsibility collide. Right now it is easy to know that my kids come first; I wish I could say it is always that clear. And yes, I did say "mother." Surely there is one, but I don't know a father who feels guilty going to work when his kid has a 104 fever.

June 23, 2009

Kathi walks in from her two days off to see that Francoise has gotten her back-room people to move all the china she worked so hard to shelve onto the end caps. Apparently, Francoise thought this was important, so that we could try to sell the shelves the china was on—twenty-five-year-old, rickety wooden things worth about sixty bucks apiece. Nuclear war is about to break out over this critical issue. Several people tell me that it will be a long time before they feel like they can be friends with Francoise because of this sort of thing. She is just trying to power through getting things done. At this point, I really do think everyone is just doing the best that they can. Francoise gets so much more done than a normal human being, partly because she cares about doing it more than about how anyone is going to feel about it.

June 25, 2009

Finally back at work; I cannot believe how much they have gotten done. Don sends me an email with an initial draft of our final customer letter. Although he has been in the middle of all of the Sarah–Kathi–Francoise drama, he says, "It is getting sadder to me now. Overall, I will miss this place forever no matter what I do next."

He and I start to plan our final Edish party. My plan is to go to Houston for the last week of Edish. In the past we have done Christmas parties and other events at Ken's house, sometimes doing all the cooking ourselves and sometimes buying some or getting a caterer. This just doesn't feel like the same kind of thing. When I suggest a restaurant, Don says, "The party will have a weird feeling no matter where it is. A restaurant is loud and doesn't lend itself to intimate talking, hugging, and crying. Maybe that's better! I wish we could have a memorial service for the business. It's probably too fresh and frightening to find humor and joy to share."

A memorial service is a weird but great idea.

June 26, 2009

File under things I won't miss: a Ukrainian hacker has gotten into our internal program. Why? I have no idea. Ken fixes the problem and suggests that we not pursue it any further. If we were staying in business, we would have to, but at this point we just need this to work for three more weeks. As always, I agree.

June 28, 2009

Max and Madeleine come down with 104° fevers and terrible sore throats again. Our regular doctor was out of town last time, but he is back. I call, and he says to bring them in on Monday.

June 29, 2009

Yet another strep test comes back negative for Max and Madeleine, but our doctor is convinced that they have it, so we start antibiotics, and I have the happy task of telling Lindsey that, yet again, I will not be able to come in for a few days. Cameron has come down with what he is sure is swine flu, so Lindsey and Kendall slog through by themselves. Lindsey sounds as if he is going to cry.

June 30, 2009

Max's doctor calls to tell me that he is really sorry that the other doctor didn't get back to me last time, and that his last strep test did come back positive. Oops. When I think about keeping everyone in my family quarantined for a week at the height of Edish's need for help, I want to scream. Not to mention my poor sick kids.

Yes, that is the order in which I thought about it.

July 1, 2009

Cameron is still sick but on the mend; he did not have the swine flu. When Bruce had emergency open heart surgery, almost everyone I know went to the doctor with chest pains. All of us were convinced we had advanced heart disease. The swine flu brings out something similar in people.

Lindsey and Kendall are down to selling fixtures.

July 2, 2009

Now that they're back on the mend, I send my kids to their grandparents for the day, so that I can finally go to work. Lindsey and Kendall have done a tremendous job, and things look more and more empty. Not only is lots of china missing, but fixtures are starting to go. It looks barren.

Don was supposed to send the paychecks yesterday UPS second-day air as always. He emails me with the subject line: *So Irritating It Is Funny:*

> *Francoise, in her haste to clear out everything, threw out all of the UPS express envelopes! Sheesh! The UPS driver is going to see if he has one. If not, he will bring one tomorrow, and I will have to overnight the checks.*

Kerry sends a long email to say that Francoise

has priced all the Sharpie pens at five cents, and that they have all sold, which meant he spent twenty minutes looking for one today. I know there must be a going-out-of-business manual that I should have read, but I wonder if it would cover this.

Don suggests that we have our Houston end of Edish party across the street at Palazzo's, which is the restaurant where Wynonne and I drank Bellinis last fall—a lifetime ago. The manager seems taken with the idea that a company would spend money to have a going-out-of-business party and gives us a good deal, although he makes it clear that he will not take a check.

It is Lindsey's turn to call in sick with a splitting headache. Overwhelming as the work in the shop is, I am not exactly in a position to complain.

Mr. Time-Waster sends me an email, asking if he can call to discuss something with me. I reply that I am quite busy, which is true. I do, however, have time to forward the email to Kerry and ask if I can just tell him to go to hell. Kerry says, "He will probably be very surprised that he'd be sent there, but if there is a karmic prepaid ticket to hell, he is on his way."

Since we are getting down to the wire and everyone else has mutinied, Chelby, Don's wife, takes some time off to come in and help him clear out his office, a Herculean task. True love.

July 3, 2009

Lindsey is still sick. July 4 is my daughter's favorite holiday. We always celebrate on the third with an early dinner party with close friends, a concert, and fireworks at the Canyons ski resort. We have done this since she and her brother were two. Our plan is to do the same tonight. But since Lindsey is sick, I need to go into the shop. Lindsey has covered for me so much in the last few weeks, when it has been really hard, that I cannot, or at least should not, complain.

I can't help but think about how many times someone has called in sick or called in that they were in the mental hospital (really), or just not shown up, and how often I've had to go in at the last minute. Christmas Eve, the day before Thanksgiving, the one and only time we had a professional family portrait, and many family events. I will miss so many things when Edish is done, but being where the buck stops will not be one of them.

I leave early. My husband has done childcare and party prep, and the day is saved.

July 6, 2009

Still no Lindsey, and my laptop monitor dies. The timing is just over-the-top terrible. Had it waited a few weeks, I could have gotten by with no laptop or taken my time to buy a new one. Two hundred and fifty dollars is what it will cost to fix. The new laptop I buy is a little more than twice that. In spite of the fact that I am a mogul and president of a major Internet company (for one more week), new computers are not my forte. My darling husband, seeing my head spin, transfers the things I need from my old laptop to new one. It takes some getting used to, as I find out the hard way in a few days.

July 8, 2009

Leaving Trevor a message that I am coming to town next week, I ask about the possibility of visiting his mother in prison. His response is puzzling. He says they are getting close to an appeal and may have good news shortly. This is a young man who went to an Ivy League college and has been nothing but smart and polite in every interaction we have ever had. I assume he is just trying not to lose hope.

July 9, 2009

The serial time-waster has sent several emails asking me to call him. I have stuck to my guns and just said that I am too busy. I do not have forty minutes to give him free advice right now, especially if he doesn't want to warn me ahead of time about the topic. Finally he emails me to ask for what he wants:

> I know that you're busy winding down your sale, so I'll make this brief. As you know, we are a company trying to do what you did so well for over twenty-five years. As you also know, it's pretty hard to compete with the elephant in the room, Replacements, and as such any help we can get is tremendously appreciated.
>
> I was wondering, if perhaps your company has some lists or databases that were not sold and as you are closing shop are prepared to throw out, it would be possible to give them to us. Two I have in mind in particular are your photo database and a list of your suppliers (which would be greatly beneficial to them as well, as we could be a new market for them). I would offer to pay for them, it's just we're not in a position at this time to justify any such expenses. What I can do is assure you that, if they come to be of use to us, we will make sure to remember you as well.

Yes, I will be sure to give you, the person who pretended to be interested in buying our business so you could get free advice, something that Replacements, which has always been nothing but good to us, is willing to pay for.

Remember how I have a new laptop? It is smaller than my old one, and I guess the touch-pad is more sensitive than the old one, too. Have you ever heard that you can retrieve emails that you sent by mistake? I have heard that too, but no one I know, including my genius husband, Kathi, or Ken knows how. How do I know this? What I meant to do was forward the above email to Ken with the subject line *Do You Believe the Balls On This Guy?* I hit *Reply* instead and sent that message. I was mortified. I don't even *talk* like that. Much.

On the bright side, I never heard from him again.

Don and I go back and forth about what we are now referring to as the Edish wake. We want it to be nice but not cost a fortune. Suddenly everyone wants to bring a date. I email all of the Houston employees:

> *Wow. I would like to take a moment to thank you for working so incredibly hard to get us to the finish line. I am overwhelmed by how hard every one of you has worked. We are planning a good bye party on Thursday, July 16, at Palazzo Restaurant at 7 p.m. Don will be handing out invitations. We are inviting all Edish employees and their significant others (and one*

young adult, Francoise's daughter). We are plan-
ning on doing the party in a small room at the
restaurant so we can all socialize, but this does
limit how many people we can invite. If you have
someone that you feel strongly about bringing,
please let me know. I would love it if you would
bring any old photos or stories to share—unless
they are bad photos of me. I really hope everyone
can come.

AARON ANNOUNCES TO the group that he is not
coming if his girlfriend can't come. I hear a rumor
about Jamario feeling the same way—Jamario, who
has shipped more china than Carter has little liver
pills. I email him that, if he wants to bring a harem,
we will figure it out; and I tell Aaron that he can
bring a date, too. Kathi, Don, and I then have a
huge fight about who gets to skip the party to make
room for the dates. We all want to; instead, we decide to squeeze everyone in.

Have you heard this? Don emails. There is a
rumor that the Harts are getting out of jail due to
judicial misconduct. More rumors fly—that there
will, or will not, be a retrial; that they are getting
out tonight or tomorrow; that they will be in the
Pavilion tomorrow; that they will never be allowed
back in the building. I cannot find a thing about it
in the papers online—until 7 p.m. Only, only, only

in Texas.

The Harts have been granted a retrial and will be out on bail until it happens. Part of the issue seems to be that the judge discussed the sentencing with another judge. As someone with no experience with this sort of thing, I don't really understand why getting advice from another person in your field about a monumental decision is a bad thing, but as usual, no one asked me. The main reason seems to be that the foreman of the grand jury that indicted them was caught on tape talking to a private detective about the case (a no-no in and of itself), saying, "I was the foreman of the grand jury, and it's my signature that indicted him." He went on to say that he had been a customer of theirs. "I bought stuff there. I sold stuff there, but one incident that particularly pisses me off, galls me, was probably in the middle to late '8os," he said on the tape. He said that he felt that he did not get paid as much as he should have at one of their auctions. "I must admit I took some glee in signing that indictment." At least one judge in Texas still thinks that perhaps the foreman of the grand jury that indicts someone should not have a grudge against that person.

When I briefly speak with Trevor, he tells me that his mother is getting out by midnight tonight.

July 10, 2009

In the Salt Lake store, we have been packing china for days to donate it to a charity. As they are carting away the last of it, we get the final retail value: $70,000. In the meantime, Don has been working on doing the same thing in Houston.

July 11, 2009

Don emails me that the packing is going well and that he doesn't have time to be emailing me.

July 12, 2009

Don calls me to say that they have gotten all of the china packed up. An old customer (she has been a customer for a long time, she is not old), Helen, came in to volunteer to help. She took a photo of the last piece of china ever to get packed. Don cried, and so did she. I am so glad I was not there. Helen also announced that she would like to have a dinner party for the Edish gang, which she later did.

Chapter Ten

"My life has been nothing but a failure." [12]

—*Claude Monet*

July 13, 2009

On the plane I think about how strange it is to think that this is the last time I will be arriving in Houston when there is an Edish. I think about all the times I have done this, including the one when my twins were four months old. I flew alone, except for them. To get through security, I had to take them out of the stroller, ask strangers to hold them, and put the stroller on the security belt. I gate-checked the stroller, and it didn't make it onto the plane. It is a physical impossibility to carry two babies and all of their stuff through an airport. Don, who was meeting me, had been able to talk his way to the gate, or we would still be there.

I kept them in a playpen at work. Everyone spent so much time cooing at them, no work got done. But Kathi took my all-time favorite photo of them: Madeleine has her little foot smooshed up against Max's face. Poor kid. Story of his life.

Walking into the shop is surreal. The china has been packed and donated. Between that and the sales since the last time I was in Houston, over a million dollars' worth of china has vanished. I knew it would be like this, so I can't say that I am surprised exactly, but it is shocking to see. The other dealers in the Antique Pavilion look at me with sad smiles. I am not used to being the object of pity and don't particularly like it. All that is left are a few empty fixtures. Sarah hugs me. So does Kerry. Francoise does, too. She looks as if she is going to cry.

I have given some thought to how I want to get through this, and I don't want to cry. Aaron and Jamario are sitting in the back, looking sullen. By virtue of the fact that they are young and strong, they have gotten stuck with lots of activities that involve moving heavy objects in Houston's ninety-nine-degree weather. The combination of that, and the fact that this is their third-to-last day of work, don't do much to cheer them up.

Kathi is being a superstar. She is hustling to get all the computers taken down. Chelby has taken yet another day off from work to help Don clean out his office. He has all the records for the last hundred years, because it is his job and because he is a pack rat. Chelby has taken on this gargantuan task with great cheer.

I am so wound up about the things I need to get done that I barely say hello. Everyone else in the room has had time to get used to seeing the shop and stockroom this empty. It takes me a few minutes to acclimate. Kerry jokes that we need to have a managers' meeting. For once, there is nothing left to say. He proudly shows me his new insurance card. His significant other has gotten him on his insurance. This is big news, since we will not be able to COBRA. In spite of the fact that we have been paying our insurance company for decades, once we go out of business, the employees have no option to continue insurance since our company will no longer exist. Even our insurance agent was shocked to hear that.

Tensions are high. Everyone seems to think someone should be doing something differently.

Trevor stops by. When I ask about his parents, he asks if I have called his mother, which I haven't, so he gives me her number. She doesn't answer when I call. Later, when she calls me back, she tells me that she is not answering calls unless she knows who it is. We agree to have lunch the next day; I offer to meet her somewhere, since I know that her presence in the building is controversial. She insists on coming to get me but agrees to come to our back entrance.

Don and Chelby and I decide to go to Palazzo after work and test out wine and appetizers for the Edish wake.

Leaving at the end of the day is odd. There isn't much to count out in the cash drawer, since all we are selling is fixtures. And everyone else in the building keeps giving me that weird, sad smile.

Don, Chelby, and I sit at the bar and try the calamari and wine, because there is nothing we won't do for Edish. In a fit of selflessness, Don tests the martinis. Suddenly I feel like I have lead in my veins. I haven't had a hard day, but I feel as if I have. We call it an early night, maybe for the first time in history, and I go home to Ken and Gary's and go to bed.

July 14, 2009

Today is the second-to-last-day of Edish: more packing things up and cleaning out the office. Kathi and Sarah are really stressed, because there is still a lot to do. A lady who has been buying up our old fixtures comes to buy most of the rest. I can't imagine why she wants them, but I try to talk her into our old Xerox machine and phone system, to no avail. I later find out from Cathy Kay that she is buying them on the sly for a woman who owns another antique mall. I cannot imagine why this is a big secret.

Wynonne calls, and I meet her outside. We go to Café Adobe, a Houston institution. She wants to go there because they have a patio, so she can smoke. If I had known we would be lunching in a sauna, I would've worn a bathing suit.

Considering everything she has been through, she looks good. No drinking or smoking for eighty days has its advantages. The prison stories are not shocking, except that she is telling them. She tells me that everyone in jail is innocent and rolls her eyes. The guards are tough, but she understands why on some level. There are lots of people who were on meth, who are missing teeth and just shake and scratch. Having heard through the grapevine that she called her son collect all day long, I am not surprised when she tells me that part of the reason was that there were many people that she came into contact with whose families did not know that they were in prison. She got her son to call the families of several people to let them know.

Her husband had it much rougher than she did. He was in state prison much of the time, and there was no air conditioning. Although he was able to buy a fan from the commissary, she tells me that many people can't afford to. Jerry got quite ill in prison; she is worried about him. I know this, not only because she tells me, but because, when he calls her during lunch, she speaks to him very sweetly, something I have never heard her do before.

The women use Skittles for eye shadow and cut their hair with razors. According to her son, she showed up at her first appeal hearing with her hair in little braids. "Mother, a sixty-year-old white woman has no business wearing corn rows," he told her.

Expecting to get probation that day, she had been shocked when she was led away after the sentencing. They are probably getting a new trial, and she seems optimistic. Although that doesn't seem realistic to me, I have no idea. Certainly, if anyone had told me that I would be lunching with her today, I would not have believed it. She seems scattered but okay. We go back to the Antique Pavilion, and she comes through our door to say hi to some of my employees.

The look on everyone's face is worth the price of lunch. One of the dealers (a friend of mine) comes into our stockroom and looks as if she might pass out. Wynonne shoots the breeze with the Edish gang for a while, then hugs everyone good-bye.

Back to my own problems. Amy, a lovely woman who works for David Lackey, comes to get Francoise because someone is out front with a truckload of china to sell. My guess is that this sort of thing has been going on regularly. Part of me wants to scream, "Excuse me, she is still on the Edish clock—not to mention that, a few short months ago, David looked me in the eye and assured me that he would never go into the china business, and he has not told me otherwise." Being exceptionally well bred, thanks to my mother, I do not.

Francoise looks at me uncomfortably and asks if I mind. Yes, I do! I scream. In my *head*. In my out-loud voice, I tell her that it is fine.

Don has finally rolled in to work and is slogging away on calling in payroll and cleaning out his office. He had car trouble, which everyone finds irritating. I can only assume that they want me to fire him.

Kathi is valiantly taking apart computers and packing them up. Our plan is to store various documents in Ken's attic, so I am pressuring Don to hurry and get everything in boxes because, like everyone else, I would much prefer to have Jamario and Aaron help me put those boxes in the attic than do it myself. Jamario and Aaron are doing the twenty-something equivalent of tapping their fingernails, texting like crazy.

Don loves pressure from me. He responds to it as well as a menopausal woman with broken air conditioning having a hot flash. A good time is had by all.

Finally it is time to go. Gary, Mathilde, and I go to dinner at the Rajun Cajun, where Mathilde and I make a spectacle of ourselves drinking beer and eating several pounds of crawfish. This is usually one of my favorite activities—both the crawfish-and-beer part and the part where I get to watch my friend with impeccable manners elbow deep in peppery shellfish. Tonight, it doesn't cheer me up.

July 15, 2009

I feel as if I'm in the last episode of a sitcom that has gone on for years, the episode where they are moving, so the house is empty, and the last person to leave looks around one final time and sees flashbacks of the kids when they were young, and all the funny and poignant things that happened to each of them. I can picture Don and me, seventeen years ago, carefully mapping out our space to figure out the maximum number of shelves we could fit, measuring our old shelves and our new space, and figuring out how to have everything made in the cheapest way possible. We were young, thin, tan, and optimistic. There was a time when no one in the Antique Pavilion looked at me as if they felt sorry for me.

I remember interviewing Kerry with Don. For the first interview, he brought his resume, which showed all of his retail experience, Neiman's, various high-end men's stores, etc. When we called him back for his second interview, he brought his resume with all of his volunteer experience. That one made it obvious that he was gay. Later, he told us that, since it was clear that Don was gay, he knew it would be okay. We loved that. Or at least I did.

I can recall talking on the phone to Bruce, when we were first falling in love, hiding in the now-vanished china aisles. That was before I could even envision a place called Salt Lake City, much less marriage, laundry, and twins. My heart would pound any time someone told me he was on the phone. Of course, it still does.

I remember huge shouting matches among Kerry, Don, Francoise, and me, although for the life of me, I can't remember what one of them was about.

We were always laughing. At the beginning of

the merger in 1999, when I came to Houston for six weeks, I was trying to save money, so I rented the cheapest car I could find, which was from some no-name agency. It broke down four times in those six weeks. I can see the Western Union telegram that Don and the Edish gang sent me the day of my Martha Stewart appearance, wishing me luck, and all of us piling together for photos with our favorite china pattern for one of our brochures (at a time when we had money for brochures). I picture Jerry Hart walking past our aisles in the early days of the Antique Pavilion with so much confidence. He was a celebrity, and the fact that he stopped to talk to us seemed just a little magical.

I remember Mildred, the cake lady who would sell home-made banana pudding, pecan pies, and cakes to us and then spend every last dime of her earnings on Royal Albert Old Country Roses. It didn't matter what kind of day you were having; a little cake and a big smile from Mildred would fix it. She'd say, "Come on, baby—if you don't have the money, just take this one."

We had a customer who used to come in to buy expensive German china with his wife, who now comes with his girlfriend. His ex-wife comes with her new husband. Richard, an elderly Chinese man, used to come in every Sunday to shop with his wife. He cared about objects more than anything, had a fabulous eye, and only bought the best. One day he told Don and me that his wife had died and he just didn't care about stuff anymore. We were so worried about him. Within a year, he had married an incredibly dynamic Chinese woman less than five feet tall with the best shoes I have ever seen. We saw her several times a week for years after that and never saw her in the same pair twice. She swore that she used to live next to Freddy Mercury in London, and that there was no way he was gay. When she referred to Richard's sons, she called them the number-one son and the number-two son, and meant it.

I am reminded of the photographer from *Southern Living* and the startled customer who got her photo in the magazine, the *Newsweek* photographer (I felt famous that day, too), the *New York Times* article, the day after Christmas (oh, yes, we all worked the day after Christmas)—when I asked Jack Kay how his holiday had been, and he said, "Miriam, Christmas is like sex. Even if it's just average, it's pretty damn good."

And of the years we had chip@edish.com as an email address for customer issues. We just loved the idea that someone named Chip worked in a china shop. When people wrote to Chip, whoever answered would sign his name. Sometimes people called and asked for him; Craig always replied,

"Speaking."

All the people who asked, "If you sell it for thirty dollars, will you pay me thirty dollars for it?"

I remember telling Kathi, Don, and Francoise that someday we would have Edish stores all around the county, and that they would be able work at whatever store they wanted. I remember telling Ken that someday we would go public.

Kathi spends much of her day trying to hurry Don along. So do I. That, of course, works really well. I want to get boxes in Ken's attic, and Kathi can't take the last two computers apart until Don is done. We get it all done sometime after six. My triumph for this, our very last day, is that I do not cry.

Leonard, Dave, Chelby, Don, and I pile into Leonard's truck and head down to Galveston. I have not been there since before Hurricane Ike. That was nearly a year ago, and I am surprised by how much debris is still there. Major gas stations still have blown-out signs; many buildings are not yet repaired. Dave points out the high-water mark on the downtown buildings, well above the second floor. Even though we reach the beach slightly after sunset, heavy machinery is still in use in a seemingly futile attempt to reclaim the beach from the sea. It seems fitting to be looking at all of this destruction tonight.

Chelby and I swim in the Gulf of Mexico while the boys drink beer and wait patiently for us. We have fancy appetizers of Cheetos and Bugles. Because two of us are officially unemployed as of tomorrow, we splurge on the nicest dinner I have ever had in Galveston, at a Greek restaurant we have to ourselves due to a combination of the late hour, the economy, and Ike. The waiters are in black suits, white shirts, and ties. Chelby and I have nappy beach hair. We have a nice bottle of wine and wonderful food. When our waiter mentions that he plays the piano at Sunday brunch, we prevail upon him to serenade us. It is a sublime evening. We are going out in style.

July 16, 2009

The day after. I go into the shop because, though we no longer have employees, there are still things to be done. Don has left me a big note taped to one of the few tables that remain, saying how magical last night was. This is true, but I think it might be an awkward thing for anyone else to read that we had an enchanted evening on the last day of everyone's job. I pocket the note. Since I can't stand to be there alone for long, I leave as soon as I can and go to work on my toast for tonight's wake.

Ken, Gary, and Mathilde come with me to the party. It is a little uncomfortable; we are all trying to be nice, but it is hard to know what to say. Don and Chelby are, characteristically, an hour late, which is making all of us cranky. Naturally, the reason they are late is that they have been working (with Leonard and Dave) on a fabulous scrapbook for me of various Edish memorabilia.

Don makes a toast: "We always joked about what we did and how it wasn't brain surgery or rocket science, but deep down I think we all knew there was something special about our work. I know I did. It was somewhat indefinable, but it is what made us come in every day and work so hard . . .just to sell teacups and plates.

"I think I finally figured it out while we were closing. We worked in a dish museum. (Maybe if we'd been a little less like a museum and more like a store, we would still be in business!) And what a museum we were. . .the kind in which, if you see something you like, you pay for it and take it home with you!"

We worked in a depository for objects that represented hundreds of years of art and technology and, more importantly, human spirit and personal memories. We were the stewards and shopkeepers of tens of thousands of tiny important things, things important to someone even if they didn't buy them. Our customers always knew where they could get the pieces they needed. Maybe we did our job too well. I think people actually thought that our shelves were their satellite butler's pantry that they could go to forever.

Our packages left the shop and went home with our customers, and we don't know exactly what happened after that. I'm sure it varied; some went into the dishwasher immediately and were used for the next day's breakfast. Some were carefully hand washed and put away to bring out for the next special occasion—a holiday, a special guest, an anniversary, a birth, a death. . . a new job.

The point is, the items we sold became part of a person's intimate life and even beyond into their legacy. The pieces meant so much more than other purchases that were here today and gone tomorrow, like a loaf of bread, or a pair of jeans or even a new car.

It is amazing how an old 1950s Noritake soup bowl means something to a lot of people. It could be the one piece that was broken in a move from the set that a family may never use but proudly displays in a china cabinet, a set that a father or grandfather brought back from overseas when he came home from military service.

A Metlox or Franciscan piece may be only valued at ten or twenty dollars, but it might go to a set that someone's mother served them dinner on every night of their entire childhood and young adult life. Not to mention that the pieces were hand painted in the 1950s by an individual who was out West living the American Dream.

This is why I think what we did was important.

I wish for Edish, the business, to rest in peace. And I wish for all the people who gave Edish its life to go forward and give their amazing spirit to their families and friends and neighbors and their coworkers at the next business where they are employed.

"THANK YOU!"

I stand up. "Fourscore and seven years ago. . . . Okay. First, I would like to say that, in the last several months, I have spent a lot of time thinking about the things I could've done differently. The things I could have done to make the business profitable. I would like to apologize for not doing them. I am very sorry.

"Of course it is much more appealing to think about the things I did well, so I have been dwelling on those. The thing I was best at was getting and keeping great people.

"When Kathi started here—wait, let me tell you about her interview. She was just a baby at the time. She came in with a leather motorcycle jacket, a plethora of piercings, and a friend. Her friend interrupted the interview to ask if Kathi had any cigarettes. Kathi was hired to be the shipper. Until recently, she was the best damn shipper we ever had—not because she had had any experience with shipping, but because anything she does, she does really well. When we hired her, back in the Stone Age, I was one of the few people I knew who had a computer. It was a black-and-white Macintosh PowerBook, for those of you who were wondering. And no, I did not play Pong on it. Back then, she did not even have a computer. She never took a computer class, but you all know what she did for us (until yesterday). She learned all about computers and excelled at it. Because that is how she is.

"Francoise was hired to be the dishwasher. She was the best damn dishwasher there ever was. Later she was the best buyer we ever had. I am including myself and David in that assessment. And Craig, but don't tell him. Although she didn't know a thing about china when we hired her, she knew how to work like a ball of fire; she is incredible.

"When David hired Don—"

David Lackey stands up and interrupts. I can only imagine what is going to come out of his mouth. He says, "When I hired Don, a lot of people in town thought I did it because he had such a great ass. And he did!" Everyone laughs hard, even Don, because it is true and perfect timing.

I go on, "When David hired Don, David told me that his sales doubled. Don was David's first employee. He was hired to ship and to sell. He was not hired to do payroll, advertising, write articles, and so on. Yet, say what you will about Don, you will notice that you never missed getting a pay-check—including the time he had to stop at Edish on his way to his father's funeral to call in payroll.

"Kathi told me that, if you read the raves sec-tion of our website, you would find virtually every employee mentioned. When was the last time you wrote a company to tell them how great they were? When was the last time you wrote a company to tell them how great their shipping was? Jamario got fan mail all the time—not because he was an ex-pert china shipper before we hired him, but because he makes sure that everything he does is done right. I would also like to point out that he does this with an extreme minimum of drama, which I appreciate. I cannot imagine how we would have made it through the last six months without Jamario.

"Jobs selling records and rubber stamps might not typically prepare one for running the sales floor of a china shop, but again, we go back to the theme of excellence. Sarah, as far as I can tell, does not give a crap about china, but she truly, madly, deeply cares that the customers have a great experience. And that everything is done right. And if Sarah does it, it is.

"Rebecca actually does care about china. And she is extremely knowledgeable about dishes. She loves them, and it always showed in her ability to sell. She also always went the extra mile, giving me great suggestions for how to improve the business. If I had taken them, we wouldn't be having this lovely dinner, though.

"Claudia is an eBay genius. And wildly self-motivated, which is a good thing, because you sure didn't get much help from me.

"Rose can take a dusty old chamber pot and a Fostoria American top hat and make them look like they are in a store on Fifth Avenue.

"Dale is another person who always cared deeply about the product and the customers. Although he and Bob were both part time, they were consistently at the top of the heap in terms of sales. Don asked Bob once why he always sold so much more out of the cases than anyone else. Bob then quietly explained his closely held secret: He goes over to the cases and shows customers the things in them. Although Bob's selling prowess is legendary, his constant good cheer was even more welcome.

"Kerry was hired to sell. And sell. And sell. He taught me the fine art of up-selling. As in, 'Would you like fries with that?' But of course he went on to do bids, not only with intelligence, but with a patience and fortitude that I can only admire from afar as he smiles at the third person this week who wants to know, if we sell it for twenty-five dollars, why we won't pay him twenty-five for it.

"And then there is Aaron, whom we kept around for comic relief. A little youthful enthusiasm sure helped lighten the mood—for everyone but Kerry. Aaron is very bright. He was hired to be the dishwasher/pricer and was quickly promoted to buyer. He accomplished, in a few short months, what took Francoise ten years." (Everyone laughed, including Francoise.)

"Don has said, 'Every once in a while, you get a do-over, and it is very cool.' We got a do-over with Vanessa, and Vanessa got one with us, and we are all better off for it. We would have been toast without Leonard's and Vanessa's help these last few months!"

"Every Edish elf is somewhere between irritated and furious with another Edish elf right now. This has been an incredibly stressful, hard thing we have done. Each of you in your own way is a perfectionist. This fact has been our greatest asset and biggest challenge. I suggest that part of the reason for the strong emotions is that each of you cares deeply about your job and making sure that it is done well. This is not exactly a bad thing.

"Kathi and I marveled at the hundreds of kind

emails that we got from customers. There must have been at least thirty that said some variation of 'When one door closes, another opens.' We were feeling like our butts were black and blue from all of those slamming doors. But I think it is true. And I know that each of you will take that passion for excellence to your next endeavor, and you will soar. Just don't forget me when you are rich and famous. It really has been an honor to work with each of you."

We drink, eat pizza, and hug. Aaron and Sylvia (a great part timer) give me very sweet greeting cards.

I do not cry.

June 17, 2009

On my way to the airport, David calls to say that he honestly hadn't seen the need for a party but now he is glad that we did it.

I buy a lottery ticket (they don't sell those in Utah), thinking what a great end to this story winning the lottery would be.

Instead, I got to go home and clear out the Salt Lake store with a little extra help from Lindsey, Kendall, and Cameron. I know it wasn't very nice, but I just couldn't bear another wake.

Postscript

> "My people owned a bit of Oklahoma
> land which would not have supported a
> pair of dieting prairie dogs. They sold it.
> The next owners dug and struck oil. They
> became Oil Millionaires. We had been
> Oil Millionaires without the use of our
> Millions because we were unaware of the
> old beneath our land. Dig and strike your
> gusher of Joy, Be the Joy Millionaire that
> you are. And spend it, Brother, spend
> it!"
>
> —Don Blanding

IF IT'S PRETTY clear what I lost, what did I find? The obvious answer emerges in the form of the hundreds of people who called, came into the shop, and emailed us. Their response is what inspired me to write this book. From the moment we sent the first email, it was clear that we had hit a nerve. The messages of support were overwhelming; so too were the number of people who just wanted us to know that we were not alone, that they were living through or had survived similar experiences. Yes, this is my story—but it is the story of many others as well.

Chuck Lorre, creator and executive producer of *The Big Bang Theory, Two and Half Men*, and a bunch of other great shows, writes something on the vanity cards at the end of each of his sitcoms. In January of 2012 he wrote Number 371 for *Two and Half Men*:

> Sometimes when I drive past a small retail establishment that is going out of business, I'm struck by an overpowering wave of sadness. I can't help but imagine what the people involved must have felt like when they opened the doors for the first time. The sense of excitement and hope that came after that first sale. The feeling that their fledgling, street-front enterprise was the beginning of a grand, money-making empire. I still have memories of the excitement and optimism that rippled through my family when my dad opened his little luncheonette some fifty years ago. All things were possible and there was no inkling that small eateries like his were soon to be extinct. *(If you were born after 1970 feel free to take a mo-*

ment and google "luncheonette.") Anyway, I guess that's the reason I've always preferred to pay a few more bucks and buy something from a struggling mom and pop shop, rather than a big chain store. Speaking of big chain stores, I also feel a wave of sadness when I click my TV remote past NBC.

Another thing I found—being fiercely angry with someone does not preclude caring for or loving them. *Cognitive dissonance* is the psychological term for it; reading about it is one thing, living with all its contradictions quite another.

As you now know, all the people who worked for me behaved with an astounding degree of grace most of the time. They were not the only ones.

When I told Tony (our Lake Powell friend) that we were closing, the first thing he asked was if I needed money. My mother did the same thing.

A woman I barely knew got in my car at school pickup and listened to me whine for twenty minutes. She's a shrink, and we are now close friends. I need a shrink friend desperately.

I found that lots of people, family, friends, acquaintances, strangers, will step up to help when asked and often when not.

My father, our friend Jon, and my husband built our kids a tree house with $10.00 worth of materials from the recycle center. The twins and their friends have had no end of fun in it. Recently, I watched my kids and their cousin walk past all of their toys and towards two empty boxes. They tied a rope to them and had their cousin pull them around in the boxes for forty-five minutes. People say that the upside of the recession is that our society is becoming less materialistic and more focused on what really matters. They may be right. Our family is making do with a little bit less and enjoying it more.

Because of Edish, I've always had a fancy teapot. Now I have time for tea parties with my daughter and her friends. I'm working on enjoying these moments with my kids—without multi-tasking. We play cards, do homework, hike, throw a football, all without me checking my emails or taking business calls.

An afternoon latte from the Starbucks down the street from Edish used be a daily treat. These days, I make my own. My cups are prettier anyway.

I also found that sometimes it is wonderful to be wrong. Craig and Ian got married and are living happily ever after in London.

Recently I was snowshoeing again, alone, with the crunch of snow beneath my feet and the louder sound of my thoughts bouncing around in my head. I was contemplating Ralph Waldo Emerson's remark "What lies behind us and what lies before us are tiny matters compared to what lies within us." As I came out of some trees, I looked up to see my first-ever snow-bow. It hadn't snowed in twelve hours, and the sky was mostly clear, but it looked as if there were snow particles in the air, and a full-on arched snow-bow suddenly appeared. It was yellow, orange, and green; the colors were more pastel than a rainbow and just amazing. Apparently they are rare. After dropping my kids off at school that morning, I had felt like going home and putting my head back under the covers; instead, I got myself moving. The snow-bow would have been there regardless of whether or not I was. I wonder what else is just waiting for me. I hope I have the moxie to get out from under the covers and go out and find it.

Endnotes

1. The title of an advertisement for Santa Anitaware. *The Best of Collectible Dinnerware*

2. *The Cocktail Hour: One Man's Strong and Unyielding Opinions*, by Don Browne (see Appendix 1). Believe it or not, I have spent many cocktail hours at Don's house that fit this persnickety description perfectly. He truly means it.

3. *China and Glass in America 1880–1989*, by Charles Venable

4. Emilio Pucci, *A Renaissance in Fashion*. Although Emilio Pucci is famous for his wild clothing prints, he also designed several patterns for Rosenthal China, not to mention flight-attendant uniforms for both Braniff and Qantas (the latter included a matching bikini), possibly the outfit Marilyn Monroe wore to her grave, a Lincoln Continental, and much, much more. He was also quoted as saying, "I am the first member of my family to work in a thousand years," but that didn't really seem like the right way to start Chapter Four.

5. In a naked (and unsuccessful) attempt to do something about our lagging cup and saucer sales, Don wrote the article for the website to be found in Appendix 2.

6. Raymond Loewy designed the Studebaker Starliner Coupe, the Coke bottle, the Lucky Strike package, and many Rosenthal china patterns.

7. Oscar Wilde supposedly said this in college. If he didn't, he should have.

8. Eva Zeisel designed china patterns for Castleton, Hall-craft, and Red Wing, and designed patterns for Crate and Barrel and Design Within Reach until her death in 2011 at 103.

9. The website is *http://bccp.lbl.gov/gta.html*. This is one of those weird china rumors that turns out to be true. A *New Yorker* article was written in 1991 about an artist who got into trouble with the NRC for buying up red Fiesta (which actually always looked orange to me). There are YouTube videos of people using Geiger counters to show how radioactive it is.

10. *Collectors Encyclopedia of Russel Wright*, by Ann Kerr, p.20. Wright and his wife Mary designed many china, dinnerware, melamine, crystal, and glass patterns, as well as furniture, wooden decorative objects, school desks, fabric, clocks, and more.

11. Rockwell Kent designed the Salamina and Our America patterns for Vernon Kilns, as well as a pattern based on Melville's *Moby Dick*. He was a writer and artist. He was blacklisted by HUAC. If you want

to know more about him, there is a PBS documentary on his fascinating life. One of the many supercool gifts that David Lackey gave me over the years was a small Rockwell Kent etching.

12. Guess it had a different ring to it when he said it. Besides creating a few paintings, he designed my favorite china pattern. Although I usually mix and match like crazy, Monet, by Charles Field Haviland, is the only pattern I own a full set of.

13. "Joy is an Inside Job," by Don Blanding. Blanding designed Hawaiian-themed patterns for Vernon Kilns. He was an artist, poet, writer, soldier, set designer, and inventor of a holiday called Lei Day, and he apparently saved the life of the then-seven-year-old Lucille "Billie" Cassin, who later went on to change her name to Joan Crawford.

Appendix 1

The Cocktail Hour: One Man's Strong and Unyielding Opinions

By Don Browne

NO DRINKING EXPERIENCE quite compares to participation in the formal cocktail hour. The only thing "formal" about the cocktail hour is that there are a few traditional guidelines that should be adhered to. Otherwise, it is time to relax and unwind from life's taxing demands.

The cocktail hour should begin at approximately 6:00 p.m. Typically, the cocktail hour (which may be slightly varied and/or extended) is what precedes the evening meal. Reservations for dinner are made (or dinner is served) around 7:30 or 8:00 p.m. Thus, dinner plans prohibit time for an extensive drink list. Complex drink experimentation is not appropriate during the cocktail hour.

The cocktail hour can best be enjoyed at home,

because the drinking activity and interpersonal exchange is meant to be an intimate experience. A bar or restaurant with no distractions will do if there is no other choice. Things that one will want to avoid in a public space are bright lighting, a television, loud and/or inappropriate music, video games, and too many other people. Having the cocktail hour at home puts the host in control of the surroundings, the company, and of course the making of the drinks.

There are a few basic tried and true classic cocktails that will do a wonderful job of giving definition to the end of one's workday while simultaneously signifying the beginning of the evening. The evening is one's personal time for rejuvenation. During the cocktail hour, tomorrow is another day.

If one has all the items needed to prepare and serve the drinks that follow, there is no doubt that a successful cocktail hour can be achieved. However, there are some other appropriate elements that are crucial to elevate the experience to perfection.

While the drinks should be good and stiff during the cocktail hour, everything else should be soft and comforting. The lighting in the room needs to be low, the seating upholstered, and the air temperature adjusted to provide relief from the weather outside. The temperature in the room should not ever be too warm; the cocktail hour is not a time to be sluggish or lethargic. Music is played an unobtrusive level but is chosen carefully to provide an invigorating mood and encourage spirited conversation. (American jazz from the 1930s through the 1960s is always appropriate).

Simple hors d'oeuvres like cheeses, patés, olives, and crackers may be offered. The entire party should not number more than six or eight people, although fewer are preferable. Guests may be old friends or new ones, but an interesting, witty, good-looking group is best. The host is always attentive to the needs of the guests but maintains a low profile.

The cocktail hour, when organized according to these traditional specifications, is frequently a near-magical time. No other brief social experience is quite like it. The drinks, the food, the music, and even the intimate conversation of companions can meld to form a perfect human experience. Even if one chooses to discuss the shortcomings of the day, it will be done in the past tense, and tomorrow is in the future. For that hour it should seem as if there is nothing else that anyone could possibly need or anywhere else that they would rather be.

The handful of very basic classic cocktails that follow should be in everyone's drink-mixing repertoire. These classic cocktails can be easily mastered before delving into more exotic libations. One should keep in mind that no other beverages are necessary for the traditional cocktail hour; this list is sufficient. These drinks should always be "made to order," never in advance. Recipes follow.

Another point to keep in mind is that the most important element in the host's satisfaction of the cocktail hour is the process. Drinks should be savored from beginning to end. The fine crystal and appropriate bar accoutrements, the best ingredients, and the creative energy result in the production and presentation of a refreshing beverage that looks and feels beautiful is the real joy.

BASIC CLASSICS
Martini (Gin or Vodka)
Gin and Tonic
Gin and Soda
Vodka Tonic
Vodka Soda
Scotch (neat, rocks, or mixed with soda or
water)
Bourbon (neat, rocks or mixed with water)

GUIDELINES FOR MIXING
The recipes that follow are given in general form. Individual tastes and glass sizes vary so much that strict quantities and measurements are not possible. The mixing of drinks is much like fol-

lowing recipes in food preparation. There are countless recipes to achieve basically the same end result. The inexperienced host should plan to do some drink-mixing experimentation prior to hosting a party. One's own taste and creativity are what will result in a great drink.

Proportions of alcohol mixers are up to the host, or the request of the guest. When more exact quantities are important in a recipe they will be given as a ratio. (For example, two parts tequila, one part lime juice, one part triple sec.) Some guidelines follow for basic types of alcohol servings:

1. Served on ice, mixed with soda, tonic, juice, or cola.
2. Served straight on ice or mixed with water.
3. Served straight up—mixed ice cold but with no ice.
4. Served neat. No mixer, straight liquor. No ice. Room temperature.

In general, when preparing cocktails on ice, mixed with soda, tonic, juices, or cola, there is a general mixing rule. Use a highball or old-fashioned glass and fill completely with ice first. The liquor is then poured to fill about one-third to one-half of the glass. Fill the glass the rest of the way nearly to the top with the mixer. Leave just a little

room in the glass for stirring the drink and for garnish. The cocktail should taste mostly like the
mixer and garnish.

Most scotch whiskey drinkers, bourbon
whiskey drinkers, and vodka drinkers who request
their drink straight on ice or mixed with water will,
however, expect to taste the liquor. Pour these
drinks in the following way. Fill an old-fashioned
about one-fourth to one-third full of ice; then pour
in enough liquor to completely cover the ice for a
straight drink. If water is requested for the mixer,
pour in enough to fill the glass about two-thirds
full. There is usually no garnish when serving
these drinks.

Drinks that are served straight up (ice cold, but
no ice) are prepared in a cocktail shaker or a mixing
pitcher. It is essential to the taste of these drinks
that they be served ice cold but not be diluted by
the ice. The quantity of ingredients used for these
drinks is completely dependent on the size of the
glass that will be used. Use a long-stem martini
glass (liquor cocktail, or sherbet/champagne) for
these drinks. Fill the cocktail shaker to about two-
thirds full with fresh ice. Pour enough liquor and
mixer that it will completely fill the glass to be used
into the shaker and shake vigorously for approximately thirty seconds. Fill the glass by pouring the
contents through the shaker's strainer opening,

leaving room only for the garnish. Serve immediately. Do not reuse the ice.

A drink served neat is a drink of alcohol that is served right out of the bottle into the glass with no mixer, no garnish, and no ice. Use an old-fashioned glass for serving this type of drink. Simply pour the requested liquor into the glass about one-fourth to one-third full, and serve.

Recipes

Gin Martini: The traditional martini is made with gin and is served straight up. Typically the gin martini is garnished with olives.

> Gin
> Dry Vermouth (only a few drops)
> Olive

Vodka Martini: This version has been popular since the 1950s (it was James Bond's favorite). Garnish with lemon or lime and serve straight up.

> Vodka
> Dry Vermouth (only a few drops)
> Lime or lemon twist.

The following four cocktails are simple basics but important because they are requested over and over again. All of these are warm-weather fa-

vorites, since they are so fragrant, icy, and tall.
Two or more lime wedges gives these drinks an
extra citrus kick that everyone seems to enjoy.

GIN (OR VODKA) AND TONIC
Gin or Vodka
Tonic Water
Lime wedges

GIN (OR VODKA) AND SODA
Gin or Vodka
Soda Water
Lime Wedges

More very simple, honest drinks that round out
the most basic cocktail-hour drink repertoire.

SCOTCH (OR BOURBON) AND SODA
Scotch or Bourbon
Soda
Lemon or lime wedge(s)

SCOTCH (OR BOURBON) AND WATER
Scotch or Bourbon
Water

SCOTCH (OR BOURBON) NEAT
Scotch or Bourbon

The next section is devoted to cocktails with a few more ingredients. These are still relatively simple drinks, but offer more exotic flavors and colors to please guests. Perhaps only one or two should be available as a "special" drink at the cocktail hour. These cocktails are especially nice to serve for variety at larger gatherings or at theme or holiday parties.

Other Basic And Exotic Recipes

CAPE COD

A great-looking, refreshing drink that one can easily picture Northerners drinking all afternoon while they relax on the decks of their summer homes.

> *Vodka*
> *Cranberry juice*
> *Lime wedges*

GREYHOUND

Fresh-squeezed juice makes this a heavenly concoction. Try it with ruby red grapefruit juice.

> *Vodka*
> *Grapefruit juice*
> *Lime Garnish*

MARGARITA

This is now the most popular mixed drink in the U.S. Delicious and potent, it is best served on ice with salt, or straight up with salt.

> *Tequila, 2 or 3 parts*
> *Triple Sec, 1.5 to 2 parts*
> *Lime juice (fresh squeezed only, no exceptions),*
> *   1 to 1.5 parts*
> *Salt*

This cocktail is an exception to the "make each drink to order" rule. Large pitchers mixed ahead of time will help to even out the unpredictable tart sourness of the limes being used. For an on-ice Margarita, start by dipping the rim of a highball glass in lime juice and then in salt. Fill the glass with ice, pour the pre-made mixture from the pitcher, and garnish with a lime slice. For a straight-up Margarita, prepare a stemmed Martini glass or old-fashioned with salt as above, Next, shake the Margarita on ice, strain from the shaker into the glass, and garnish with a slice of lime.

TEQUILA SUNRISE

This is an absolutely delicious drink, and one that looks as good as it tastes.

> *Tequila*
> *Orange juice*

Grenadine
Citrus slice
Maraschino cherry

It is important that the grenadine be added to this cocktail last. Pour tequila over ice, then almost completely fill the glass with orange juice. Quickly add a dash or two of grenadine, which will initially sink to the bottom. Garnish the drink and watch as the grenadine gradually mixes in and floats to the top of the drink, giving the appearance of a beautiful mini-sunrise in a glass!

CHAMPAGNE COCKTAIL

There is actually no hard liquor in this one, which makes it a great, light, and bubbly concoction.

Champagne
Sugar Cube
Angostura bitters
Lemon twist

Put a sugar cube in the bottom of a stemmed martini glass. Add a dash or two of the bitters, fill with champagne, and garnish with a lemon twist.

BLOODY MARY

The absolute best hangover remedy and cocktail to accompany breakfast or brunch. These are also wonderful refreshments in anticipation of a seafood dinner.

> *Vodka or Aquavit, 1 part*
> *Tomato juice or V8 juice, 2 parts*
> *Worcestershire sauce, 1 to 3 tablespoons*
> *Cayenne pepper to taste*
> *Black pepper to taste*
> *Lime wedge(s)*
> *Pickled green beans*
> *Pitted green olives*

Fill a highball glass with ice and fill one third high with vodka. Add the Worcestershire sauce, and top off with tomato juice. Garnish with olives, limes, and pickled green beans. Sprinkle peppers on top to taste.

DAIQUIRI

This is the original that quenched the thirst of servicemen in the Spanish-American war, not the modern frozen overly sweet concoction that goes by the same name.

> *White rum*
> *Lime juice*
> *Confectioner's sugar*
> *Lime wedges*

Serve this one straight up. Fill a shaker with ice, then with liquor and fresh-squeezed lime juice in equal parts. Add 6 to 8 tablespoons of confectioner's sugar. Shake vigorously and serve in a stemmed cocktail or old-fashioned glass. Garnish with lime.

MADRAS

This cocktail is delicious served straight up or over ice. Either way, it gets the job done.

Vodka, 2 parts
Orange juice, 1 part
Cranberry juice, 1 part

TWISTED WINDEX

This is a gorgeous and tasty drink if you can get over the unlikely color.

Vodka, 2 parts
Blue Curacao, 1 part
Lemon twist

Serve this eye-popping drink straight up in a martini or champagne glass.

Appendix 2

The Mugging
of the Cup and Saucer

By Don Browne

WHAT HAS BECOME of the cup and saucer set? Why is it that people seem to use their cups and saucers less and less? Is life too short? Has modern American life really gotten so hectic that there is no time for a saucer?

Is life so different now than it was just a few years ago, when cups and saucers were a vital element in the drinking of one's tea or coffee? Has the coffee industry successfully marketed the consumption of larger and larger quantities? Are cups just too small now for the popular current appetite? Can the cup and saucer portion only be looked at now as a relic of a consumer lifestyle of yesteryear?

Today, cups and saucers are more likely to be displayed unused in a china cabinet, or put into a cup-and-saucer collection that just sits on a shelf looking beautiful.

For coffee and tea drinking, the mug (not to mention the commuter cup and to-go cup) has very nearly taken the cup and saucer's place.

The evolution of size, style, color, and use of pieces of china is a natural one. The mug, relatively recently introduced, is a welcome addition to the china repertoire. The mug has its place and is a wonderful thing indeed, but it is not a replacement for the cup and saucer! Ironically, there are more reasons and occasions now than ever to use them.

To start with, a typical cup in a cup and saucer set holds about 8 ounces, while a mug generally holds about 12. Health and dietary issues, including caffeine intake, are a primary concern for many Americans. Switching from mugs back to cups and saucers is one simple way to trim caffeine intake by twenty-five percent!

Although an increasing trend in coffee consumption in recent years has consistently been toward quality not quantity, there are those who are drinking more coffee than ever. Most of the wonderful high quality designer/gourmet coffees that are prepared at home are not only fresher and more flavorful, but stronger and much more expensive. Instead of using a mug, the slightly smaller cup-and-saucer-size portion is perfectly appropriate to

use for such wonderful, rich coffee. Coffee has tra-
ditionally been served in smaller portions after dinner, so a mug is definitely not an appropriate
option. The after-dinner, or demitasse, size cups
and saucers are the perfect option. After all, as the
name indicates, they were designed especially for
service at this time.

Since most individuals do not have after-dinner
cups and saucers in their patterns, the regular cup
and saucer is the next best choice. Besides, good-
quality decaffeinated coffee is now so readily available that guests wishing to limit their late night
intake of caffeine could still enjoy a full-size cup.

What about tea? Americans appear to be increasing their tea consumption, although much of
the tea consumption is of the iced variety (an en-
tirely different subject). Traditional afternoon
English tea is also gaining wider American popu-
larity. Since so many major European-style hotels,
and some restaurants, have started to offer teas,
many individuals have started to follow suit at
home. Regardless of quantity, most would have to
agree that it is only fitting to have one's tea from a
cup and saucer, not a mug.

This brings up another point—the overall propriety of the cup and saucer. Propriety for its own
sake has historically been of little interest to Americans. However, there are some things that have

preserved a standard because they really cannot be improved upon. Undoubtedly, the wonderful, en-hanced tactile experience gained by using a cup and saucer is one of those things. Many generations have maintained the tradition, which supports the idea that it must be worth the tiny bit of extra ef-fort.

The point is that cups and saucers still have their place and always will!

At the Salt Lake City store, looking natural

Bob and Tonia Clark in their house, with Max and Madeleine

Chelby with Madeleine on our pre-Ike fishing trip

China Beach

Craig as a blonde

Don and Lisa, a former employee, at the Houston store

Early photo of Don and me

Gary and me at Lake Powell—notice the snow-covered mountains in the background

Gary, left, and Ken

Leonard and Dave

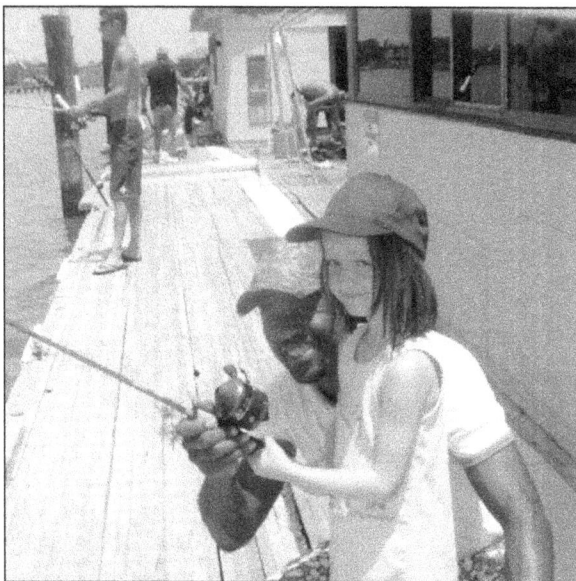

Leonard fishing with my daughter

Mathilde, with Madeleine and Max

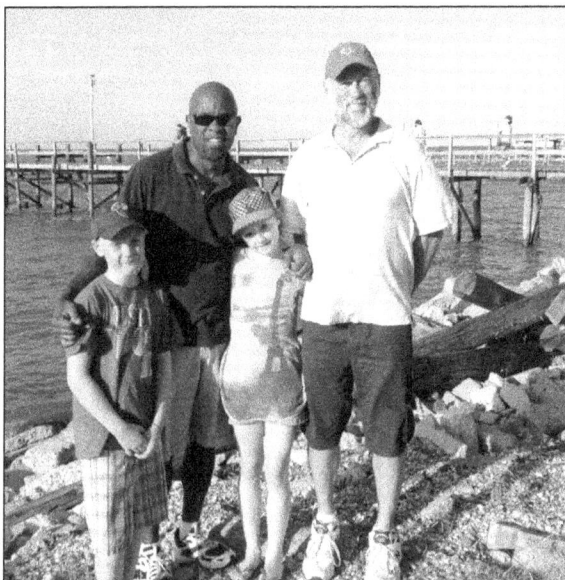

Leonard, left, and Dave, right, with Max and Madeleine

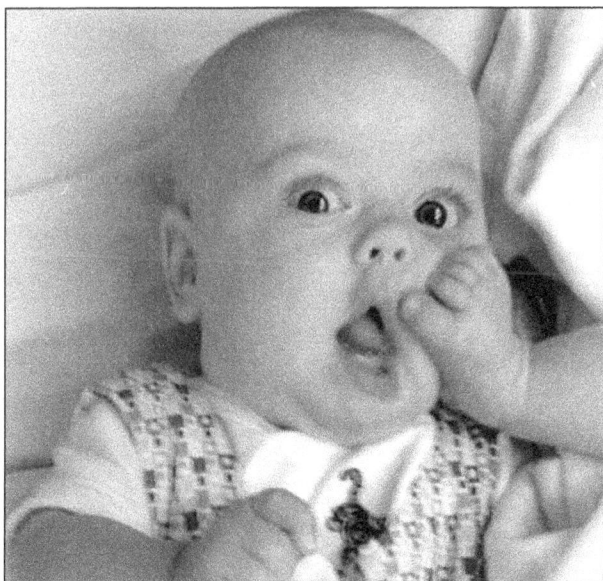

Max, and Madeleine's foot

www.ingramcontent.com/pod-product-compliance
Lightning Source LLC
Chambersburg PA
CBHW030822090426
42737CB00009B/827